PR
GREAT WORK

Crowell's inviting guide helps turn overcommitted, exhausted readers into productive and engaged dream-followers.

—BookLife Reviews

The world of work is changing, and Dr. Crowell's strategies give us the advantage we need to end up on top.

—KEVIN HARRINGTON, The Original Shark from ABC's *Shark Tank*

Amanda Crowell's *Great Work* is a guide to achieving a meaningful career based on one's personal, distinctive talents.

—*Foreword* Clarion Reviews

Dr. Amanda Crowell's strategies have the power to change lives.

—JOE THEISMANN, World Champion Quarterback and Entrepreneur

We all have something keeping us from becoming our most fulfilled selves, claims cognitive psychologist and coach, Amanda Crowell. Here, she explores how to discover one's own "Great Work," and then achieve it.

—*BlueInk* Review

In *Great Work*, Crowell re-acquaints us with the work we love best, re-ignites our passion for the work that we value above all else, and gives us a practical framework to ensure we actually get to do that work. I am forever changed by Crowell's insights and inspired by her doable strategies for freeing up precious time to do meaningful work that matters.

—AJ HARPER, Author of *Write a Must-Read*,
Editor & Publishing Strategist

Whether you are trying to figure out what your Great Work is or have already been doing your own Great Work for many years, you will undoubtedly benefit from reading this book!

—DYAN DENAPOLI, Penguin expert
and author of *The Great Penguin Rescue*

In a world of "get happy" quick schemes, programs, and books, Amanda stops to ask "But what is your great work?" In a way that's both fun and meaningful, practical and inspiring, prophetic and present—*Great Work* will help your up level your experience of yourself.

—MIKE GANINO, Creator of The Mike Drop Method,
Celebrity Public Speaking Coach

Dr. Amanda Crowell's strategies are a powerful combination of high-octane motivation and proven tips that will change your life.

—PATTY AUBERY, President, Jack Canfield Companies;
Past President, *Chicken Soup For the Soul* Books

A must-read for anyone who wants more out of life, and feels like they are being passed by as they work harder and harder without getting to where they want to be.

—JULIE ELLIS, Author of *Big Gorgeous Goals*, Keynote Speaker, Leadership Coach and Co-Founder of Mabel's Labels

Crowell's approachable, engaging style encourages us to exchange our distracted worries for what makes us feel alive. This work is a rallying call and armament for us to make a difference, be authentic, and do Great Work.

—DR. MEGHAN BATHGATE, Director of Educational Program Assessment at the Yale Poorvu Center for Teaching and Learning

Great Work was a great read, from start to finish. I encourage anyone who wonders how to leave a legacy, or who wants to enjoy their time at work more, to read this book.

—MICHELLE ARPIN-BEGINA, Founder and Chief Behavioral Officer of Michelle AB

Dr. Amanda Crowell's book, *Great Work*, has provided the blueprint for where I need to focus my time and effort on what I feel called to do… my own "Great Work"!

—MATTHEW KUSZA, Founder of Mythos Creative Writing

GREAT
WORK

DO WHAT MATTERS MOST
WITHOUT SACRIFICING
EVERYTHING ELSE

AMANDA CROWELL, PhD

For David,
who believes before I do,
supports without fail,
and pushes me to keep going when
doubt and worry crowd my mind.
True love lasts a lifetime.

CONTENTS

INTRODUCTION

"What am I going to do?"

As the other seventy people left the webinar, Beatrice waited silently. Finally, as the last person logged out, Beatrice asked her simple question.

"What *am* I going to do?" she said again, this time mostly to herself.

Beatrice had just attended an hour-long presentation focused on how to do the work that matters the most to you—what I call Great Work. One of the activities we do is The Project Audit, a rough assessment of how many projects an attendee is trying to cram into their life at one time. The numbers can be *staggering*. Fifteen or twenty projects is on the low end; some discover that they are trying to manage fifty or sixty different projects at the same time.

The Project Audit regularly stops people in their tracks. When you are juggling sixty projects, it becomes clear why the most important ones aren't gaining traction. Beatrice, it turns out, was keeping forty-five projects going. She was running her own coaching business, managing the backend of her husband's creative agency, renovating her house in preparation to sell it, and taking care of her aging mother. Though she was exhausted, she was keeping these projects afloat through sheer force of will.

What she wasn't keeping afloat was her Great Work. Great Work is my term for the work that matters the most to you. We often think of it as our life's purpose and, sadly, it's usually the first thing to go when we get busy, or life becomes complicated. This is certainly what happened to Beatrice. She was not writing her book or launching her group coaching program, two projects that excited her and would have taken her coaching practice to the next level. Beatrice knew that if she could just get her ideas organized, she could move from a one-to-one coaching model to a one-to-many coaching model. This would pave the way for more impact and more money, two things she badly wanted. And yet, there simply wasn't time.

Beatrice understood she wasn't prioritizing her Great Work, but she felt that she had no choice; everything else felt entirely non-negotiable.

"Everybody needs me," Beatrice explained. "My husband can't stay on top of his company without me, my brothers and sisters live out of state, and we need to sell our house because we just can't afford it. And now there's a pandemic, which has made it all worse… and I'm at my wit's end. In fact, the only thing I *can* let go of is my Great Work, and I really don't want to do that. I just don't see another option."

Beatrice—a beautiful, fierce, powerful woman, who is admired by all who meet her—put her face in her hands in despair.

"I'm so tired, Amanda. I just don't think I can do all of this." She looked up and I got the sense that she would be crying if she was sure that she could stop.

This was one time when the webinar format just didn't hold up to an in-person event. I wanted to put my hand on her shoulder and really look into her eyes. Instead, I leaned forward and looked directly into the camera.

"Beatrice. I promise, you don't have to do it all. There is another way."

Beatrice puts her heart and soul into everything she does. She is driven and focused and a great coach. The problem is, she spreads herself too thinly. She struggles to say "no" when someone else needs help, rarely delegates, and because she doesn't want other people to know how hard things have gotten, she almost never asks for help. Beatrice is deeply committed to her family and to growing her coaching business. There is no question that if she knew a way to do it all, she would.

And I know exactly how she feels. I created the Great Work Method because I simply couldn't keep up with everything I "had" to do, let alone find time for what I *wanted* to do. I began to worry that I would never write the books calling me from the inside, deliver the workshops that I knew would help other people, or speak at least once on a really big stage. All of this so I could respond to a tsunami of emails and attend a lot of meetings. I began to have an existential crisis: *Would I go through my whole life and never get to my Great Work?*

I thought that if I could just work harder, be more efficient, and stop procrastinating, then I could finally get to what mattered. This was how I had earned my success, after all. There was no way I could afford to pay for college, so I went "over and above" in high school and got a full scholarship to a local, private university. I worked harder and faster than most other people and earned my PhD from an Ivy League school in four years, where the average completion timeline is seven years. I moved my family halfway across the country to pursue a prestigious post-doctoral fellowship while caring for an infant and finishing my dissertation. At every turn, I worked as hard as was humanly possible, and I succeeded beyond anything that was ever expected of me.

And yet, succeeding through brute force turned out to be a losing battle long-term. I couldn't stay ahead of my own ambition and drive; I was my own worst enemy. The more efficient I got, the more I took on. The more I took on, the more exhausted I became, and suddenly I was back to seeking even more efficiency. It wasn't long before I was as efficient as I could possibly be while still being healthy. Then I "had" to dig into the time I used for sleep, exercise, health, fun, creativity, and joy. Before long, even that was not enough.

There is an inconvenient, but incontrovertible truth here: There will always be more that we could, should, and must do, than there will be time to do it.

This truth found me cycling between two settings: I was either striving so hard on so many projects that I drove myself to the brink of exhaustion, or so desperately trying to recover from overworking and burnout that I slipped into patterns of avoidance and procrastination. I call this the Productivity Roller Coaster of Doom and it's no fun at all.

To stabilize my own experience, I turned to my obsessive researcher tendencies, honed from decades as a cognitive psychologist. Drawing ideas from across traditional time management methods, brain science, mindset research, burnout prevention tactics, change management processes, and behavioral change theories, I experimented on myself relentlessly. Out of this process of trial and error came a potent combination of research, strategies, and tactics that allowed me first to slow the Productivity Roller Coaster of Doom, and eventually get off entirely.

I no longer worked every night and weekend. Instead, I painted, napped, played with my children, and read novels again. I was more energized and less distracted, which made my work better and made me happier. By doing less and making time for fun I became, without a doubt, a better writer, coach, and educator, not to mention a better friend, mother, and partner.

It worked so well, in fact, that I started sharing these ideas with my clients. My clients are universally high achievers, passionately seeking to make a difference in the world with their work. They, like me, were daunted by the sheer number of things they were already doing—let alone the endless projects, collaborations, and responsibilities they could take on. And, like me, they needed support and encouragement to shift focus to their health, happiness, and to their Great Work. I was happy to discover that the Great Work Method worked for them, too.

- One client finally completed her licensing paperwork and exam in three months, a project that had been hanging over her head for ten years.
- Several clients found the courage to start their own businesses, after years of waiting to be "ready."
- Many of them wrote books, launched podcasts, started blogging, and discovered that sharing their unique perspective felt wonderful.

- Quite a few of them found new roles or new jobs that aligned with their vision, furthered their Great Work, and made them feel happier.

They discovered that what had felt impossible, was in fact more possible than they could have hoped. And all of this happened while they felt better, more grounded, joyful, and invigorated. This is because Great Work flows better when we are happier and healthier.

Turns out, when we commit to doing much less and then align our time to our Great Work, good things begin to happen. As we do less, we stop living on fumes, and start to feel energized and excited about our lives again. Prioritizing health and happiness allows us to be more creative, think more quickly, and be better collaborators. Figuring out how to do the work that lights us up from the inside, that draws upon our natural interests and passions, and comes from our unique point of view, feels sensational.

After discovering that these ideas worked not just for me, but also for my clients, I crafted a series of journals to help create the habits outlined in this book. The *Great Work Journals*[1] are used by people around the world to create healthier habits (*The Great Work Journal*), build their businesses (*The Great Work Journal for Entrepreneurs*), and finish their educations (*The Great Work Journal for Students*). The demand has been strong, which leads me to believe that we are not alone, you and I. Lots of us are desperate to *finally* get to our Great Work in a way that doesn't require that we sacrifice everything else.

Beatrice and I spoke about four times over the next year. She agreed be a part of a pilot group for the *Great Work Journal*, and she checked in with me regularly and let me know how it was going. There were hard moments, like when Beatrice told her husband that he needed to find someone else to do his books. And relieving moments, like when she found a woman at her church who would take her mother out for walks a couple of times a week. And exciting moments, like when she launched a small cohort of her group coaching program. She's doing her Great Work! And she's not sacrificing everything else.

Beatrice told me, "I'm happier than I've been in a long time."

One of the things I hear most often from people who have had success with this method, is how much better they feel, almost immediately. Even before they really start to make progress on their Great Work, the process of rolling back their overcommitments (though difficult!) can result in an overwhelming feeling of relief. And doing even a little bit of our Great Work can be so invigorating and energizing that it can feel like a new lease on life.

Even though the impact can be felt almost immediately, it can still be extremely difficult to convince people to give it a try. The promise that you can do the work that matters without sacrificing everything else can feel like a dangerous lie. Many of us have spent most of our adult lives being rewarded for hard work that goes above and beyond, receiving compliments and praise for our hustle, commitment, and willingness to go all out for the team. It can be very confronting to hear that our "success at all costs" work style might be optional, even when that same work style is crushing our spirit, delaying our Great Work, and harming our health.

Michael, a lawyer at a mid-sized law firm in Texas, heard me talking about time management and burnout prevention on a podcast a few years ago. He was working around the clock trying to make partner and hearing these ideas made him outright angry. He shared his reaction with me in an email.

"It just felt like a fairy tale. I knew, in my bones, that to succeed I had to work harder than anyone else. I had to show up early, work late, and meet every opportunity with enthusiasm. I thought that burnout was for losers. People who couldn't hack it. People who didn't have what it took to succeed.

"I thought about that interview a lot over the last couple of years. I can't tell you when I switched from being angry to considering that you might be a little bit right... but I do remember when I decided to take it seriously.

"I fell asleep on the couch in my office for two days in a row as I was working on a case. When I finally dragged myself home on the third day, I discovered that the water had been running in my bathroom sink for two days. I must have wandered off when I was done shaving. I was probably on my phone responding to email.

"Water had flowed out of the bathroom and more than halfway into my bedroom, ruining the carpet. I could already smell mold. I sat down on the bed in my crumpled suit and just stared at the ruined floor, too exhausted even to wrap my head around who to call. Then my phone rang. It was a partner at my law firm telling me she'd found an error in my work, and I was going to have to redo some of it.

"I heard your voice in my head right then saying that even when we think we can do the impossible, the day will come where we realize that we haven't really done it. We've made mistakes on things that matter, ignored things until they blow up on us, or let our health get so bad that we have to stop everything to

recover. This was my rock bottom. I looked up your website, saw the journal you made, and I've been using it ever since."

Michael wrote this email to me after to me after he had made some serious progress. He took a vacation for the first time in three years (thankfully returning home just before everyone got locked down for the COVID pandemic), ended his workday by seven p.m., and began exercising more regularly. Basically, he made space for his health and happiness in addition to accomplishment and success.

> *"Imagine my surprise when I heard you on a podcast for lawyers recently! You were talking about how Great Work tends to flow better when we're healthy and happy... and you know what? I think you're right. It wasn't until I had gotten those crazy hours under control, and figured out how to take better care of myself, that I started to take on pro bono work again. I suddenly remembered why I had become a lawyer in the first place."*

Michael was not alone in his initial rejection of the Great Work Method. I get *plenty* of pushback. Most of the advice you'll hear about productivity aligns with Michael's experience. According to the world at large, the keys to success are hard work, commitment, willpower, and discipline.

And these things do matter!

You will struggle to be successful if you won't work hard, aren't committed, and don't have the willpower and discipline to keep going in the face of challenge. But these are not usually the struggles of those of us yearning to do Great Work.

Our problem is on the opposite end of the spectrum. For us, it's very easy to take things like willpower and discipline too far. We hustle beyond the point of healthy. We push through our natural breaking points until we are thoroughly burned out. And, we say "yes" to so many things that the important ones get put on hold.

It's hard to deny that people can be very successful by pushing as hard as they can and "dominating" through "hustle." There are examples of this everywhere. But what my clients and I have discovered has also become hard to deny: *There is another way.*

You can do Great Work that feels good, prioritizes what matters to you, and maintains space for your happiness and health, all while still meeting your most important obligations and responsibilities.

This book provides a blueprint for this other way. I'm here to promise that you can figure out what your Great Work is, align your time to it, and make remarkable progress *without* overworking. And all three parts of this promise matter!

- Making progress without a clear idea of where you're headed is an exercise in futility and can be a source of great frustration.
- At the same time, it doesn't help to figure out what your Great Work is if you can't move it forward!
- And it's definitely not worth it to pursue Great Work at the expense of your happiness and health.

In order to experience the benefits of the Great Work Method, you will have to change how you spend your actual time. You will need to do things differently in the hours and minutes of your life. To make progress on stalled projects, like Beatrice, you need to roll back your commitments and ask for help. To re-invigorate your passion, like Michael, you need to set some boundaries and make time for your health. And if you want to get off the Productivity Roller Coaster of Doom, like me, you need to build in regular time for fun, recovery, and creativity, not just striving and accomplishment.

When you do these things, you'll experience a change that goes far beyond how you spend your time. This work will impact your passion, your relationships, and your career—because how we spend our time is how we spend our lives.

CHAPTER ONE

THE CALL TO GREAT WORK

If you do not change direction,
you may end up where you are heading.

Attributed to Lao Tzu, an ancient Chinese philosopher,
founder of Taoism and author of Tao Te Ching

ONE SATURDAY MORNING SEVERAL YEARS ago, I woke up late following a frantic week at work. My body hurt. My head hurt. I felt as though I hadn't slept at all. My thoughts picked up right where they had left off the night before: "I can't go on like this...."

My life had gone completely off the rails. I worked late nights, early mornings, all through lunch, and every weekend. I hadn't taken a day off, including weekends, for at least two months, and I was behind on three big projects.

I was in real trouble.

Mean Amanda, the critical voice in my head, started in with her litany of shame: *You suck. You don't do enough. You aren't smart enough. You were deluded to think you had what it takes to make a difference.* I squeezed my eyes shut, turned over in my bed, and buried my head in the pillow.

Through the fog of shame, I heard my children laughing downstairs. "No, Daddy! You're silly!"

I groaned. "Oh, no. I have to go down there and be cheerful."

I dragged myself downstairs to do my duties: Feed the kids, talk to my husband, make the grocery list. I didn't *want* to do any of it. My husband, David, was holding court in the kitchen, annoyingly perky in his workout clothes, waiting for me to emerge so he could go to the gym.

"Mommy!" my daughter, Abi, cheered from behind an enormous blueberry muffin.

"Good morning," I said, hating myself for my obvious lack of enthusiasm. I poured myself some coffee and glanced at David. "Must be nice to go to the gym."

"You can go to the gym. When I get back, just go."

"I'm not going to the gym, David. There's too much to do! I have to finish that report this weekend, and we have to grocery shop and do laundry. All so that we can go back to work next week and do it all again."

David's eyes narrowed. "So, you don't want me to go to the gym."

At my husband's now-sharp voice, I felt panic rise in my chest. And then, a stabbing feeling right in the center. I grabbed my chest, gasping.

"What? What's wrong?"

"I don't know. I've never ... GAH," I put both hands on the table and leaned over. "My chest hurts."

"What did you eat? Is it heartburn?"

"I don't know! I had what you had. What did we eat?" I dropped to the floor, pushing my sweaty palms against my racing heart. I looked at David, scared. "Am I having a heart attack?"

All four of us piled into the car, David and I trying to appear normal so the kids wouldn't be afraid. As we drove to the hospital, I did my best to ignore the sounds of the *SpongeBob SquarePants* theme song drifting from the back seat.

All I could think was that despite four university degrees and a willingness to sacrifice everything—including my health and happiness—*I didn't have what it takes.* And it broke my heart, because what I wanted most in the world was to make a difference with my work. I wanted to be the boots on the ground, bringing my passion and perspective to schools.

When I was offered a job at a consulting firm that focused on improving educational outcomes for students who were at risk of dropping out, I was very excited. This company was doing important work in *real* schools, impacting *real* teachers, and *real* kids. The opportunity to join the movement toward better schools was why I had gone to graduate school.

This was a chance to do some of my Great Work. Work that was engrossing and important, grounded in my unique gifts, and offered to the world with a sincere desire to make a positive difference.

And I blew it.

Tears streamed down my face; I turned toward the window so the kids wouldn't see.

We pulled up to the ER. I wiped my face, turned toward my husband, and noticed for the first time how worried he looked.

"Call me as soon as you know something," he said.

When you tell an ER nurse that you're thirty-six and think you're having a heart attack, you get processed quickly. With an efficiency I hadn't anticipated, they drew my blood and hooked me up to a heart monitor in thirty minutes flat.

"Don't think about anything stressful," the nurse said. "Lie quietly and just breathe."

Just breathe? When was the last time I had done that? Certainly not at all in the last four months! When you do consulting in schools, spring is *intense*. Spring, which used to be my favorite time of year—previously the season of flowers and baby chicks—transformed into the season of stress eating, tension headaches, and panic, as all my many projects rush to finish before the end of the fiscal year. And because I worked in a company with intense feedback protocols—where every email, agenda, and slide deck had to be approved before it could go out—the workload became nearly impossible.

"Why is your heart beating faster all of a sudden? What are you thinking about?" the nurse asked. I snapped back to the ER.

"Sorry, I was thinking about work."

"That'll do it!" she said before leaving. "Try to stay calm. We want to see your heart rate stabilize."

Try to stay calm.

Just breathe.

Why was this so hard?

When the doctor came in, the look on her face made me sit up straight. "The good news is that your heart is strong and healthy. The bad news is that you had a panic attack. Are you under a lot of stress?"

I laughed (which did not amuse her), and then told her about my schedule and workload.

"Panic attacks are a clear red flag," she advised. "If you don't address this, it could lead to further problems—a heart attack or an autoimmune condition or an anxiety disorder... this kind of burnout is a real health concern. You need to get it under control."

She was right, of course. I had reached a state of total burnout.

Looking back over my morning pages from that time, what I see is an exhausted, over-achieving perfectionist deep in feelings of despair. After weeks of working all the time, my exhaustion was so complete that even a full night's sleep barely made a dent. I felt cynical, callous, and hopeless. I lived with the pervasive worry that I was never going to be good enough, smart enough, and committed enough to do my Great Work.

According to Christina Maslach and Michael Leiter, whose work forms the basis for almost all current theories on burnout, this is the very definition of it:

Exhaustion + cynicism + hopelessness = burnout.

And as the doctor noted, burnout is *serious*. In fact, the incidence of burnout has reached such epidemic proportions that the World Health Organization acknowledged it as a syndrome[2].

It shows up in three distinct ways: exhaustion at work and at home, cynicism and disengagement toward the people in your life, and hopelessness about whether things will ever improve. It is a miserable feeling, and if you're reading a book about not "sacrificing everything else," I'm guessing you have likely experienced something like it at least once.

That day in the ER, I realized that losing my chance to do Great Work was only part of what was on the line. If I wasn't careful, I could lose my chance to enjoy my kids when they were small. I felt dangerously close to ruining my marriage and neglecting my children. I was clearly damaging my health. Forget having fun or feeling good!

And yet, I did not know *how* to turn things around. How could I add "manage my stress" to my to-do list when I was already so completely burned out? Working harder was simply not an option; it was the grind that had landed me in the ER in the first place. How was I going to meet everyone's expectations—including my own, which were extremely high—without losing what was left of my sanity? It felt like I had to choose between my all-consuming dedication to Great Work and myself, my family, and my health.

WHAT IS GREAT WORK?

"Great Work" is the work that matters the most to you. You likely think of it as your life's purpose, and it might very well feel like your "reason for being on the planet."

As I describe it on my podcast, *Unleashing* Your *Great Work,* it's the work that emerges from your unique point of view, keeps you on your evolving edge, is done in community, and creates your legacy. Your Great Work might involve building a business, leading an innovative team, working toward a scientific discovery, raising a tight-knit family, creating world-changing art, or starting a movement.

The problem was, I didn't *want* to choose between Great Work and a good life. I wanted both.

Isn't that what we *all* want? A chance to do something important without having to sacrifice *everything else*? Was that even possible?

It was time to find out.

HOW TO DO *ALL THE THINGS* WITH LESS STRESS

I DECIDED TO START WITH what was clearly the real problem: myself. Other people at the company were not falling apart from the workload; I was obviously doing something wrong. I had lots of ideas about what that might be: If I could overcome my laziness, conquer my selfish desire for downtime, erect some solid boundaries, and stop wasting so much time on distractions like social media or Netflix, then surely, I could find a way to work hard enough to survive my ambition. I needed discipline and willpower, and I needed them now!

(You likely agree that a major part of my problem was how hard I was on myself. I expected robotic perfection in all things and berated myself for every shortcoming. But it took me another couple of years to figure that out.)

I started with traditional time-management tools from the world of "high performance"—those focusing on discipline, process, habit formation, hard work, and willpower. I happened upon David Allen's *Getting Things Done (GTD)*[3], a structured time-management system that helps you do *all the things* with less stress. The core system involves processing your workflow with the efficiency of a Japanese factory. It promises that, if you can keep your inbox at zero, maintain your systems perfectly, and never forget to write anything down, you can *do anything*.

As I learned the ins and outs of *Getting Things Done*, Kanban, Pomodoro, and time blocking, I made some incredible progress, and I learned a *lot*. These tools allowed me to move through my never-ending to-do list with comparative ease, and I ultimately found the grueling pace of consulting much less exhausting. I stopped working on weekends and falling asleep with my laptop at night, and in turn, my marriage and family life improved dramatically.

In short, I really did get a lot more done, and I really did experience less stress. My performance reviews were good, and I was no longer miserable. Win!

But even though I was tearing through my ever-growing to-do list and proving myself valuable to the team, I didn't—on the whole—feel more relaxed, grounded, or joyful. What I felt was efficient. And, somehow... that felt like enough.

Looking back, I have to wonder: *Why* did that feel like enough? Why wasn't I more concerned about the quality of my life, in addition to the quality of my work?

HOW TO LET YOUR HAPPINESS MATTER, TOO

I WAS NOT ALONE IN this quandary. Over the years, I've noticed how little we *all* seem to value our own desires and happiness. Questions such as, "Would you really enjoy that new role?" or "What about starting a business sounds exciting to you?" are often met with sentiments like, "I don't know," and "Why does that matter?"

Suggestions such as, "Maybe you should say 'no' to that promotion," or "Why don't you ask your boss if you can hand that piece of your work off?" regularly rile people up to the point of anger. The premise around that anger goes something like this: "You don't understand how much I need this job. If I disappoint people, I might lose this opportunity, and then I'll be screwed for sure."

While riled up, people will regularly point to my privilege, the success of my business, the cushiness of my job, and the fact that I have a gainfully employed husband as the reason I "can" do things like that and they "can't."

Those things are true: I do have a job I love, a business that's successful, and a husband with a good job. And I'm grateful for all those things, as well as my innate curiosity, my ability to speak and write, and the fact that I pursued a field (psychology) that I find endlessly fascinating.

But it's also true that I had the same husband, privilege, curiosity, and field when I was sitting in the ER with the weight of my commitments crushing my chest.

So, what changed? How did I go from an achievement-at-all-costs addict to someone who is at least as deeply committed to my health and happiness as I am to my Great Work?

For almost two years after that fateful trip to the ER, I stayed in consulting. I got so efficient with my time that I not only tore through my to-do list, but I also carved out time to start a side-hustle. I love teaching, coaching, mentoring, and writing, so I decided to take my extra time to do more of those things.

I began delivering workshops on psychology, sharing my action-driven approach to change that you'll see in the pages of this book. After these workshops, people began to ask me to coach them and so I did. When I moved from consulting to being a university professor, I had even more flexibility and I used that time to build a successful coaching business. It was interesting, challenging, and at times, quite overwhelming. But it never occurred to me to slow down. *If I can do it all*, I reasoned, *then I should do it all.*

And so, "do it all," I did. Well, I didn't actually do it *all*. Obviously, I didn't eat properly, exercise enough, or go on as many adventures with my family as I would have liked… but if we're talking about the "all" that is inclusive of everything that was an accomplishment tied to an expectation, or is important for professional advancement, I DID. IT. ALL.

Imagine my reaction when my body again retaliated against this superwoman complex. Almost exactly four years after that trip to the ER, every one of my major joints filled with fluid. Both knees were so full, I couldn't climb the stairs. My shoulders hurt. My ankles hurt. My wrists hurt. My back hurt.

I just hurt: everywhere.

I went to the doctor, and the diagnosis was "generalized autoimmune syndrome." Not yet fibromyalgia, or rheumatoid arthritis, or any of the other scary conditions one finds on the internet, but a clear, unadulterated, autoimmune "flare up." The doctor sucked out the fluid and put steroids in my knees, gave me a prescription for opioid pain medication, and sent me home to "see what happens."

Here's what happened: I got *scared*. Was this my life? What had I done? What was I going to do? Who was I going to ask? How long would this last? Now, I am not a medical doctor, nor do I play one on TV. I wasn't even, *until that exact moment,* someone who obsessed about food, toxins, self-care, vitamins, green smoothies, or intermittent fasting.

Who I was (and am) is someone whose father fought for his entire life against the mighty pull of opioids. He found heroin in Vietnam and died in my home, addicted to pain killers. Every minute of his life in between was dominated by opioids, leaving him broke and alone.

I was *not* taking those drugs.

Suddenly, the bargain I had struck—Great Work at the sacrifice of everything else—became untenable.

I asked every medical professional, integrative medicine doctor, alternative wellness practitioner, and health coach who stood still long enough how to stop my body from attacking itself. And in about eighteen months, I was able to calm the autoimmune response, lower my cholesterol, resolve some early heart problems, lose twenty pounds, and remove the fluid from my joints. I am healthy again, and I never took an opioid.

The advice I received from these qualified professionals ranged widely—from essential oils, meditation, and strength training to raw juices. Despite their range of solutions, there was one commonality: Every last one of them, at some point, said the same thing—"You need to manage your stress, have some fun, and stop striving so hard."

Essentially, make some damn choices, woman! Stop doing *everything.* Stop saying "yes" to "all the things" and then expecting perfection everywhere, all the time. Do less. Much, much less. And then, don't go making yourself miserable with a litany of shame and self-recrimination. Instead, do what brings you joy, creates gratitude and appreciation, and makes you laugh. Stop worrying about being everything to everyone.

I had to change my priorities.

I was certain that by pulling back and taking better care of myself, I was giving up on my Great Work. It seemed impossible that I would be able to do less, be nice to myself, and have fun while still accomplishing what mattered. The thought of giving up was so painful that I allowed things to escalate to almost life or death before I changed my behavior. At that point, I didn't feel I had a choice.

With sadness in my heart, and a pretty severe case of depression on my hands, I nonetheless forced myself to accept this truth: In the choice between health and Great Work, health had to win.

What I discovered next shocked me.

DOING GREAT WORK WITHOUT SACRIFICING EVERYTHING ELSE

IT'S BEEN SEVERAL YEARS SINCE I was diagnosed with an autoimmune disease and "gave up" on my Great Work. In the intervening years, I've done more Great Work than at any other time in my life.

I've learned, without a doubt, that my Great Work flows best in the absence of hustle. In fact, as I dedicate more of my time to maintaining my health, doing the things that bring me joy, and spending time with my family, my creativity and focus flow more and more readily.

My coaching practice fills to capacity with more ease.

I finish more creative projects more quickly.

I make more money.

I'm offered more opportunities to collaborate than ever before.

Maybe most importantly, I've settled down. My experience of work isn't all-consuming, even as my work products (blogs, products, clients, courses, etc.) have increased. The overwhelm, self-shaming, and perfectionism that used to consume me, swallowing my time in worry and fear, have eased. They are still there, popping up when something is important to me, or when I'm trying to do something I've never done before… but overworking and worrying is not my default setting anymore.

I was shocked to discover that creating some resilience— doing less, being more compassionate toward my wants and needs, and allowing time for fun—was the honest-to-God secret to unlocking my Great Work.

I started integrating what I had learned about this resilience into the action-focused coaching that is my specialty. I began urging my clients to do less, anchor into their unique perspective more, and create actual space for what matters in their lives. Just like me, when they began to pull back, prioritize, and make time and space for fun, their Great Work began to flow.

Clients began to finish projects that had stalled for decades. They started their private practices, wrote books, launched podcasts, and found new jobs. They discovered that what had felt impossible, was in fact more possible than they could have hoped. And all of this happened while they felt better, more grounded, joyful, and invigorated.

It turns out that Great Work flows better when we are healthier and happier.

GREAT WORK HELPS US
REDISCOVER WHO WE REALLY ARE

As I've worked with people to help them transition away from a pressure- and shame-filled approach to this more compassionate approach, I've watched them rediscover who they are when they aren't maxed out and living on fumes.

They rediscover that they are fun, when they've been grumpy for a decade. They rediscover that they are creative, when they haven't picked up a paintbrush in fifteen years. They rediscover that they are deeply committed to an issue or cause that they've ignored for more than five years.

In short: They come back to who they've always been but have forgotten.

In this book, I'm taking you through five steps that will help you rediscover who you are and what you want, and then support you to get those things. They are the same steps I take my clients through, and the very ones I used myself.

These are the steps that will put you on the path to Great Work:

1. **What Is Your Great Work?** Great Work is the work that matters the most to you. It feels like your purpose, and though we often try to ignore it, it simply can't be denied. No one can tell you what your purpose is—you must discover it for yourself. I'll help you do this in Chapter 2.

2. **Do Less—Much, Much Less.** To make room for what matters, you need to stop taking on so much. Doing less

will provide immediate relief and free up your mental resources for the work that matters the most to you. We'll dive into this in Chapter 3.

3. **Make Your Great Work a Reality.** Once you've made space for your Great Work, you need translate your vision into action. A vision is exciting, but transformation comes when you do real things in your real life: every quarter, every week, and every day. I'll guide you through this process in Chapter 4.

4. **Discover How You, *Specifically,* Do Great Work.** There are a lot of tips, tricks, and best practices in the world of productivity and time management. Some of them will work like a charm, and others will derail your progress. Developing your secret recipe of self-expertise is the focus of Chapter 5.

5. **Exchange Defensive Failure for Productive Failure to Do Great Work.** No matter how aligned you are, when you are doing Great Work, you are going to run into challenges. You will likely procrastinate when you should start, experience self-doubt when it's time to persist, and run into perfectionism when it's time to wrap it up. We'll talk through all of this in Chapter 6.

In short: I'll teach you how to do Great Work without sacrificing everything else.

YOUR GREAT WORK IS CALLING

IN ALL MY YEARS TALKING to people about their hopes, dreams, and plans, I've never met anyone without Great Work calling to them from the inside. I'm certain you have Great Work calling you, too.

Great Work makes your heart beat faster. It stops you in your tracks with desire for your best life. When your Great Work winks at you from across the room, you are entirely captivated.

Despite our visceral and primal reaction to the call of our Great Work, many of us have swept it aside.

The author says, "I'll write my book when I'm retired."

The artist says, "I've spent so many years training to be a lawyer; I can't just pivot and make art!"

The entrepreneur says, "I have a great job with a retirement fund. I can't risk everything to do my own thing."

The activist says, "I'm just one person; what could I really do, anyway?"

The helper says, "I'll never make enough money doing what sets my heart on fire."

I want you to know, I would never ask you to risk everything for a pivot. It's anathema to this book for you to sacrifice yourself to the issue, the business, the art, or the work.

Instead, I'm asking you to honor *who you are* by doing some of your Great Work this week. Today. And tomorrow. And next week. And then, over time, as you chip away at your Great Work, in the ever-evolving pursuit of your vision, you will be amazed by what you can accomplish.

You can do Great Work while your life stays on the rails, your family grows together, and your health is rock-solid. The same can't always be said of people who shove their Great Work away. In fact, *not* doing your Great Work can make you reactive and unhappy, causing you to develop all kinds of stress-related illnesses. Of course, doing (or not doing) your Great Work is not the only thing that impacts your relationships, health, and happiness. But it *is* a force to be reckoned with.

And why wouldn't it be?

Your Great Work is your purpose.

It's your reason for being.

Your soul's voice speaks through it.

Your heart is settled by it.

You need it.

And, frankly, you can't escape it.

I've seen people pretend that they aren't artists, entrepreneurs, activists, and helpers… and it's almost like they fade to grey. At best, they feel stifled, out of sorts, and cranky all the time. At worst, they feel anxious and depressed.

And I've seen people who feel anxious and depressed do *just a little bit* of their Great Work and start to shimmer and feel alive again.

Here's my point: When you are being called *from inside yourself* to something, then you are meant to do it.

It's *real*.

It's your birthright.

Why wait any longer to start?

Let's begin in the very next chapter.

CHAPTER TWO

WHAT IS YOUR GREAT WORK?

Tell me, what is it that you plan to do
with your one wild and precious life?

*Mary Oliver, Pulitzer Prize
and National Book Award Winning Poet*

GREAT WORK, AT ITS CORE, is very simple: It's the work that
matters the most *to you*. It excites you. It drags you out of bed,
knowing that you are living a life of purpose.

When people hear this term, they often assume I'm talking
about great works of art, very successful businesses, scientific
discoveries, or widespread fame. These accomplishments might
very well be a part of someone's Great Work, but so are lots
of other more common endeavors such as raising children,
painting handmade greeting cards, and growing the world's
largest pumpkin[4]. Great Work isn't about being great and it's not
even entirely about work, at least not in the strictly professional
sense. Instead, we are talking about those things that call to you
from *inside yourself.*

GREAT WORK

Each of us has something that call to us from the inside, that stop us in our tracks and causes us to wonder: Could I do that?

Could I be a successful speaker, coach, and author?

Could I illustrate superheroes who save the world?

Could I build a business selling gadgets that change the face of work?

Could I help reverse climate change, incite a revolution at work, or close the achievement gap?

Could I?

Could I *really*?

That right there, that voice in your head spinning those tales of impact and creation and excitement, that's the voice of your Great Work. Every time you hear it, you prick up your ears. When you see it, it catches your eye. When you see someone else doing it, you become envious.

And every time your mind wanders into the realm of day-dreams, there you are—standing on that stage, or in the shark tank pitching your great idea, or working away in your light-flooded artist's studio. Whatever your Great Work is, *there you are*, doing it.

As I've studied examples of Great Work for my podcast *Unleashing Your Great Work*, I've notice four commonalities, which I call the Essential Pillars of Great Work.

1. It emerges from your unique perspective.
2. It keeps you on your evolving edge.
3. It's done in community.
4. It generates a body of work that creates a legacy.

32

These Essential Pillars, built upon the Four Forces Framework[5] developed by Trish Blain, support us to discover and deepen our Great Work, and to help us realize that we've already been doing Great Work.

Great Work emerges from your unique perspective. It shares who you really are and what you really think. It expresses your truths, tells your stories, and shares your wisdom. So often, we say and do what is expected of us. We fear that our unique point of view will put us at odds with people we care about or reveal a part of us that feels vulnerable. Great Work asks us to share those parts of ourselves anyway, which has a surprisingly therapeutic and energizing effect on our lives. It feels good to be ourselves.

Great Work keeps you on your evolving edge. It keeps you problem-solving, figuring things out, and trying new things. This makes it both exciting and scary. I love being on my evolving edge, but it *can* be an acquired taste. Some of us can't get enough, while others need a healthy dose of self-compassion to build a habit of going out of our comfort zone. I would argue that we *all* enrich our lives when we spend at least some time on our evolving edge.

Great Work is done in community. It involves other people, whether that's asking others for help, seeking feedback, or collaborating with other experts to complete a larger project. Great Work usually can't be completed without the infusion of other perspectives. But work done in community goes beyond assistance and collaboration. There is a magic that happens when two people bring their Great Work together. Serendipity blooms, innovation flows, and the quality of work goes beyond what either individual could have done on their own.

Great Work creates a legacy. Our lives generate a body of work that contributes to the world we live in. Whether that involves a collection of books we've written, a series of policy briefs, or simply a history of emails we've sent to co-workers and friends, our work is generating our contribution to the bigger human experience. The stories we tell, the things we learn, and the collaborations that we pursue are reflected in the things we create. Great Work transforms that history into a legacy with lasting meaning, that others can build upon.

CHOOSING GREAT WORK

CHOOSING TO DO GREAT WORK requires courage, commitment, and consistent effort. And it can be a difficult choice: Sharing our truths out loud in the world for all to see is vulnerable. It's not the default path—no one chooses us for it—and it could take us somewhere completely unexpected. And yet, it's worth it because Great Work is *why we are here.*

Great Work makes life exciting. As we learn to do what we've always wanted to do, we feel alive and eager to do more.

Great Work is reassuring. In the face of unpredictable times, our Great Work reassures us that all is not lost. We are not lost. We are here, now, doing this work that matters to us.

And Great Work is powerful. When we don't know what to do, where to turn, or who to ask, we can always come back to ourselves and listen. Who am I? What do I think? What do I want to create, or say, or do, or be? And then, without waiting for permission, we can begin to get closer to it.

ALL WORK IS NOT CREATED EQUAL

BACK IN 2015, AS I was just getting started in coaching, I put together some workshops—such as "The Psychology of Change" and "Designing Your Ideal Life." I offered them at a truly remarkable place called The Brooklyn Brainery. Many people attended these workshops who were bored or disillusioned with their career and unsure about what to do next.

Chloe came to three of them, and she brought friends.

After the third workshop, she approached me and asked whether I would be willing to work with her on her career.

"I don't know why, but I think you can help me," she said.

As a new coach still figuring out what it took to get clients, this was great news! A new client? I was in!

In our first conversation, Chloe brought me up to speed on her career:

"I've worked for terrible bosses at great nonprofits. At first, I thought if I was a good enough employee, it wouldn't matter how much of a deranged micromanager my boss was. But that turned out to be false."

Chloe's first job out of college was at a nonprofit in Chicago. Her father knew someone on the board and recommended her for the job. She worked on a small team composed of herself, the executive director, and a program manager. Chloe's boss was well connected but her grasp of the day-to-day work of the organization was tenuous at best.

"Her 'great ideas' would derail us and then we'd have to manage her disappointment when they didn't work. She would rage and blame us for a week before begrudgingly 'forgiving' us. It was exhausting."

Six months before we began working together, she was offered a role doing data analytics with a strategic partner in their New York office. "At my old company, data analysis kept me out of the line of fire, so it seemed like a safe fit. The problem is that now *all I ever do* is sit in a corner and look at Excel. I refused to admit it for six months but the truth is, I'm really unhappy. I think I need to look for a new job, even though it's only been a few months."

I noticed two things about Chloe's career trajectory: First, she was having a very common experience. I say this not to devalue her struggle, but rather to acknowledge that nothing—no job, no marriage, no relationship, nor client—is ever perfect. In fact, almost everyone's first job involves boring or confusing work, difficult colleagues, and the stark realization that the world of work is not the "sterling outcome of adulthood" we hoped it would be. Some of Chloe's anguish and turmoil were coming from these difficult-but-valuable truths.

The second thing I noticed is that Chloe had no hand in either of the roles she'd held. The first one was recommended by her father, and the second involved being poached from her prior employer. Both sounded fine to her, but neither were what she would have chosen on her own. In fact, her career trajectory had almost nothing to do with her own vision for her own life; it didn't reflect her desires, her interests, or her passions at all.

I don't mean to imply that we should decide in advance which opportunities are right and then pursue them on our own, eschewing all offers of help and new ideas. Certainly not! Most of us find ourselves in roles, careers, and positions that we acquired through a combination of active seeking and serendipitous connections. In fact, it is through our networks that we acquire clients, projects, and job offers which exceed anything we could have imagined on our own. The key for Chloe, and for the rest of us, is to ensure that we are guided by a vision of our Great Work so that we can seize the opportunities that get us closer, while politely declining those opportunities that take us in an unrelated direction.

WHY WE RESIST ACKNOWLEDGING OUR GREAT WORK

"WHAT HAD YOU HOPED YOUR career would look like when you were in college?" I asked Chloe.

"Well, the main thing I need is to make enough money. And at least with this new job, the pay is high enough for me to rent an apartment here. Moving across the country wasn't cheap, and I really like New York. I'd like to stay."

Notice how she didn't answer the real question? Chloe dodged the question about her hopes, because she didn't think that her desires were particularly important when there were bills to pay. The need for enough money is as real as it gets, especially for those of us without family resources to lean on in times of transition. Fear that there won't be enough can make us blind to our own hopes, almost as though they are irrelevant. "I have actual, practical needs, Amanda! What I want is going to have to wait, because I have rent to pay."

Chloe will be a better employee, make more money, get more promotions, and be happier if she allows her hopes, dreams, and desires to play a role in what she does with her career. But does that mean she should *only* do what she's passionate about, practical bill-paying be damned? No, of course not.

Great Work, like most things, is not an all-or-nothing proposition.

We can be informed by what we want and still take a job that doesn't entirely meet those desires because it's a stepping-stone or a stopgap. We can do work that bores us for a while, so we can pay our bills while we build our skills and expertise. We can slow down and be mentored, because we need help to learn our chosen craft.

Consider this: If we take a job that bores us and we don't have a vision for our Great Work, we are inevitably going to feel stuck. But when we are guided by our Great Work—cultivating an awareness of what we want and seeking opportunities and mentors to help us get closer to those things—we feel less trapped, more creative, and more hopeful, *even though we haven't yet changed our external circumstances.* Having a strong vision changes our experience even before we change our situation. It's that powerful.

THE COMPETITIVE ADVANTAGE OF GREAT WORK

THIS PERSPECTIVE—THAT YOU SHOULD HEW closely to your Great Work—is not without its detractors. I often hear about the importance of paying your dues, doing your time, and letting experience guide you rather than your naïve interests.

There is truth in that!

I do not think that someone directly out of college or at the beginning of a career change should expect only interesting work and a lot of responsibility before he or she has the experience and expertise to do it well.

I *do* think, however, that every one of us, whether we are brand new to the workforce or fifty years in, should seek the chance to do more of our Great Work: work that matters, work that excites us, and work that acknowledges and honors *who we are*.

The work you do will be better. You'll be a better observer of yourself, your industry, and your role. You'll be a better collaborator, have better ideas, and do better work. And, you'll probably get more promotions, earn more money, and be in higher demand.

Basically, there is a powerful competitive advantage to doing what interests you!

This advantage comes from the *type* of interest and motivation you feel for your work. You see, there are two kinds (broadly speaking): intrinsic and extrinsic. Intrinsic motivation is born inside of you. It's grounded in interest, driven by curiosity, and connected to your hopes, dreams, and aspirations. This is the kind of motivation we typically feel about our Great Work.

Extrinsic motivation, on the other hand, comes from outside of you. It's grounded in expectations, tied to approval and regulation, and sometimes driven by worries, fears, and scarcity. The work we do while motivated in largely extrinsic ways is at best "fine" and at worst shallow and poorly executed.

For the sake of an example, let's talk about buying a car.

My husband recently bought a white Honda Civic. From the beginning, he was very invested in buying the "best car for him." He talked to everyone about their cars, and even took a trip to our mechanic to show him the two he was considering. He investigated the comparative upkeep of a white car versus a grey or black car (apparently, there's some kind of special wax needed). He researched, considered, compared, hemmed and hawed, and obsessed over every detail for six months before he bought his vehicle.

Why was he doing all this? Because he was intrinsically motivated. He wanted to know which options had emerged since he last purchased a car (interest). He was curious about the impact of electric and hybrid cars on mileage expectations (curiosity). And he was deeply invested in being able to pass his new car down to our children in ten years when they would need a starter vehicle (long-term hopes and dreams).

When I bought a car, I just got the same vehicle that everybody else on my block had, because they said it worked for kids. I test drove it, it seemed fine, and we took it home. (My husband was horrified.)

Who would you want in charge of buying your car? My husband, of course! He's much more likely to make better use of limited resources while making a more informed decision. And he's primed to get better and better at buying cars over time. These are the same things we are looking for in employees, and the things we want to cultivate in ourselves for our careers.

And this is why it matters that you do what interests you in your career and life.

It will simply go better.

NO ONE CAN TELL YOU WHAT YOUR GREAT WORK IS—YOU MUST DISCOVER IT FOR YOURSELF

CHLOE, LIKE SO MANY OF us, accepted whatever opportunity she received, and as a result, she found herself somewhere kind of random.

And then, after doing the work for a while, it became familiar.

And then, she got another opportunity in the same field, which gave her experience and maybe even some expertise.

And all of that felt safe.

Maybe she was meant to be there? Maybe she should just be satisfied with what she had?

One of the first steps toward our Great Work is to admit that we want *specific* things.

Things that are different from what we have.

Things that might not make sense to other people, yet.

When I asked Chloe what she wanted, she dodged the question because leaving the safe, familiar field where she was valued and had marketable skills felt entirely irrational. A change, just so she could be happier, felt like an outrageous proposition. And anyway, it probably wouldn't work.

That logic did not originate with Chloe, nor does it end with her! And it's not only an artifact of being young and underpaid. Marie, a friend of mine who has worked in talent acquisition for two decades, and whose annual compensation is around $250,000, was miserable in her career until relatively recently.

Right out of graduate school, she fell into a job with a recruiting company serving investment banks. Marie has a strong social justice orientation and was never entirely comfortable in the glitzy, high-wealth environment of investment banking. And while she's a great communicator, she didn't enjoy the production process of running through hundreds of candidates to find the best ones. Nonetheless, her strong work ethic and friendly personality meant she was good at it. She was promoted to manage larger teams and bigger contracts.

Despite all of this, she was exhausted all the time. "Being good at something is not the same as feeling good while you do it," she said.

Eventually, Marie got up the courage to ask for role outside of direct recruiting, which helped her feel a little bit better, but it wasn't until she moved out of investment banking and into the healthcare industry, that she started to *feel good* at work. "Even though I make a little less money, I don't mind. I'm working for a company that has a mission I can get behind, and I feel a lot better."

Why do so many of us struggle to make a change to get closer to what we actually want from our careers? The reasons are plentiful, and almost entirely false: We think we are too old, too young, too inexperienced, too experienced, too busy, or not busy enough to justify a scary change with no guarantee of success.

This kind of deep self-doubt leads us to make some odd choices: We entirely deny the voice we hear, calling from inside ourselves. Then, we trust other people—who aren't privy to our deepest wants and desires—to tell us which opportunities we should follow, or what career path to take. Not to mention, who to date, where to live, and which hobbies to engage in!

Now, obviously, I'm all for advice. In fact, one might say I'm in the advice business! And when it comes to *how* to get what you want, I say take *all* the advice you receive and use it to inform your self-expertise (more on this in Chapter 5). But when it comes to *what you want* (as opposed to how you get it), that really must come from inside of you.

No one can tell you what your Great Work is.

You must discover it for yourself.

FINDING THE THREAD OF YOUR GREAT WORK

I'VE FOUND THAT EVERYONE HAS something that runs through their desires—a thread that brings together our most moving experiences, feeds off our natural interests, and sparks the fire of curiosity. It's this thread that ties together our Great Work.

For some of us, that thread is situated squarely in an established career path and requires little interpretation. That describes my career in education. I wanted to help make schools better for our most vulnerable students, so I pursued a PhD, became a college professor, and I write for scholarly publication. All predictable components of this career path.

For others of us, finding their Great Work requires a little more digging because what we want is off the beaten path, or involves an unusual combination of skills. This describes my career in coaching, writing, and speaking. I want to help people pursue their brightest potential, so I offer workshops, coach people on their Great Work, and write blogs, articles, and books for the mass market. None of this make sense to other academics or teacher educators, and yet I consider it some of my Greatest Work.

In either case—whether you power down an established path, or hack your way through the jungle one step at a time—it helps to name the thread that holds your Great Work together.

HOW TO IDENTIFY A GREAT WORK THREAD

To uncover your Great Work Thread, let's start by looking at your life to see what has always been true.

What has guided your choices and made you feel alive? Have you always been committed to a particular issue? Have you always sought out the opportunity to be organized and in control? Have you always volunteered to make the posters or images for social media, or other visual artistry, even though it's not in your job description?

Or, alternatively, what feels missing? What causes you to feel envious? What part of you needs an outlet that isn't there? Is it creativity? A seat at the table? A difficult problem to solve?

Sometimes, we can find our thread by looking at the things in our life that feel like the worst fit and asking: What would be better?

Are you working in a bureaucracy and can't handle the snail-like pace? Are you doing big-picture strategy work, but love to be deep in details? Are you constantly on the phone, but yearn for silence? These are clues, too.

This can be a challenging task for some people. Chloe, for example, had a difficult time articulating her preferences and tendencies. She claimed that she was "all over the place," "enjoyed too many things," and didn't have a "clear idea of what mattered."

I didn't believe her. And I don't believe you!

No one is as unpredictable as they think; there's a Great Work Thread in all of us, and we are going to find yours.

QUESTIONS TO FIND YOUR THREAD:

What has always been true?

What has guided your choices and makes you feel alive?

What feels missing?

What causes you to feel envious of others?

What part of you needs an outlet that isn't there?

What part of your life is the *worst* fit? What would be better than that?

POSSIBLE GREAT WORK THREAD: YOUR UNIQUE WAY OF BEING

IT MIGHT BE THAT YOUR Great Work Thread is your unique way of looking at the world. You might carry a holistic view of human nature, or a deep and enduring pragmatism. Or you might see all of life as an opportunity to create.

My client, Jonathan, is an artist to his core. He drew comic books as a kid, watches art house movies, and earned a dual bachelor's degree in accounting and studio art. His charismatic personality and CPA made him an easy hire for a client-facing accounting role at a large, multinational company. He loved the paycheck and had some great friends at work, but the rules and regulations of accounting in a publicly traded company combined with the rigid structure of his company's bureaucracy made him feel completely out of place.

When we started working together, he described a pervasive, low-level depression. "I feel like a fish out of water, trying desperately to walk... but longing to swim." See what a poet he is? It wasn't until he left his large corporation and joined a boutique accounting firm for privately held companies (where regulations are much less oppressive) that he started to feel like himself again.

For Jonathan's work to feel great, he also needed an outlet for his creativity. As part of his new role, he is speaking at conferences on behalf of the company and contributing posts to their funky social media channels.

"I'm here to make the world a more unusual place, and I finally get to do some of that at work!" he shared.

GREAT WORK THREAD: ISSUES THAT MATTER

SOMETIMES, YOUR THREAD IS THE problem you want to solve. It could be that you are driven to solve climate change, cure cancer, describe history with more accuracy, or understand why (why!?!) humans are so fond of self-sabotage. The problem captivates you, and maybe it always has. You don't entirely care how you get involved, but you *must* be part of the solution.

Nazifa was someone I met when I was doing my PhD. We did a federal policy institute together, which involved traveling to DC and meeting with a bunch of education policymakers. We were there for four days, and Nazifa was like a kid at Disney World. Seeking details and examples, she had a question for every speaker. Then, she would listen with rapt attention.

One night, we found ourselves seated next to each other at dinner, and I asked her what her plans were after graduation.

She was in the policy master's program and was graduating in just a few months.

"I'm moving to DC, and I'm hoping to get a job in education policy," she said.

"Is there something specific you want to do? A job title or type of organization?"

"I don't care whether I work for the federal government, or an NGO, or a nonprofit as long as I'm helping to close the achievement gap for Black and Brown students." This is what it looks like when someone is obsessed with a problem. For Nazifa, the exact nature of the work was less important than being in conversation with the people trying to solve it.

Nazifa did move to DC and got a job at the United States Department of Education (USDOE). Her role has changed a few times in the past decade, as she moved out of the USDOE and joined a non-profit focused on using standardized testing to close the achievement gap. I reached out to her recently to ask for her permission to share her story in this book.

When I reminded her of our conversation, she said, "How funny… I don't remember that! But it's true. I mean, I care much more now about the role I'm playing in solving the problem, but my focus hasn't wavered. I feel like I was put on this Earth to raise awareness and eradicate the impact of low expectations on our most vulnerable students."

GREAT WORK THREAD: THE INDUSTRY, SECTOR, OR FIELD

FOR SOME PEOPLE, IT'S ABOUT the context of the work rather than the problem or their personal "way of being." When the context draws you, everything about it interests you. It feels interesting just to be there. This fascination with context describes a lot of people I know who work in entertainment, theater, politics, and fashion. These competitive and somewhat glitzy worlds are, for some people, endlessly fascinating. But it can also describe people who are captivated by less glamorous contexts, like schools, fishing boats, and automobile repair shops.

Leondra is endlessly fascinated by theater. Though she had no interest in being onstage, she *loved* being backstage. As a theater major in college, she enjoyed running the school productions. She began her career at a bank branch, wearing high heels and selling accounts from the glass office in the back. It was fine, but she missed the theater so much, it made her stomach hurt.

"I spent all my money on tickets to Broadway, off-Broadway, and off-off Broadway shows. I went to everything! But going to the shows was also a little depressing… I didn't want to be in the audience; I wanted to be backstage! I wanted to be a *part of it all.*"

Eventually, Leondra decided she had waited long enough: She took a second, very low-paying job working concessions at a Broadway show. She worked there for two years and made friends with *everyone.* Eventually, little opportunities came her way, and she found her way backstage. Currently, she's the production manager of a theater's off-Broadway season and couldn't be happier.

"I'm still fascinated. I get tired, don't get me wrong. Theater can be hectic and unpredictable, and I need a break like anyone else… but when that break is over, I want to come back to the theater. I don't think I'll ever get over it."

YOUR GREAT WORK THREAD MATTERS

Now, imagine if Jonathan was working in Nazifa's role, trying to nudge bureaucracies forward through carefully worded policy. Or if Leondra was in Jonathan's role, talking about accounting on stage instead of running the show backstage. Or if Nazifa was stuck backstage at a theater with no impact on the achievement gap. The mismatch would be *palpable*.

That is what we want to avoid.

Chloe, it turns out, had all three of these threads running through her, none of which were present in her then-current role.

"If you could have a job with a great commute, enough money, in an industry that excites you, doing work that matters, what would that look like?" I asked.

"Well," she said, "I was an economics major, and I have always been fascinated by corporate social responsibility. I would love to help a large, powerhouse corporation make a real impact on important issues, especially climate change. I want to have a seat at that table, working against climate change in the corporate environment."

Now we were onto something. As Chloe and I spoke more, we realized that every part of that vision spoke to her more than her current role.

- **Her unique way of being:** seated at the table, discussing and collaborating on strategy and implementation.
- **The issue that matters:** balancing the economic forces of profit and shareholder interest against the values of the organization and prevailing social forces.
- **The industry, sector, or field:** a large, profitable corporation.

Her job in a small social-service organization, working behind the scenes with other small social-service organizations, was not interesting to her. She knew the work was important, and she loved having a stable paycheck, but the rest of it? It was "fine."

I'm arguing that "fine" isn't good enough.

It doesn't make you excited.

It doesn't push you to dig in.

It doesn't make you feel alive!

And life is too short to feel bored, disengaged, and a little bit dead inside.

WHAT IF I STILL DON'T KNOW WHAT MY GREAT WORK THREAD IS?

IT'S POSSIBLE THAT JUST READING the examples of the threads above gave you the insight you needed to identify your Great Work. If that's true, then you can skip to the next section. If you are still a little unsure, or you just want some further proof before you move on, I want to suggest that we switch things up.

No more words!

It's time to turn to the visual world, where our preferences are not as hidden, and our desires aren't constantly hijacked by concerns about what's possible or reasonable before they even have a chance to be heard[6].

I want you to collect a stack of about seven or eight magazines. They don't have to be magazines you would actually read. In fact, the last time I did this exercise, I got my magazines from my physical therapist's office. He had *Time, Sports Illustrated, Popular Mechanics,* and a super-old copy of *Redbook,* none of which I read. They worked great!

Before you begin, set an intention. It might help to write it down on a Post-It that you keep visible while you are working. It can say "I'd like to see my Great Work," or "Show me my purpose," or any other words that get your head into that space. Some people like to light a candle or use aromatherapy to set the stage. If that gets you excited, do it!

When ready, give yourself about thirty minutes to tear through the magazine, pulling out things that speak to you. Don't use scissors, because they will slow you down. Just tear it out, and don't judge those craggy edges (perfection has no place in vision!).

Speaking of judgment: Don't judge any of this process! In fact, if you find yourself doing anything to disrupt this entirely visual process, like considering, comparing, or evaluating (or any other logical-sounding thoughts), move faster! Tear through the books fast enough that it shuts down the logical, conscious mind that wants to interrupt your flow.

After you've worked through the magazines, take the images you've amassed and look at them. What do you notice? What desire is staring back at you? What Great Work do you see between the lines?

Trust your instincts, here, even if it feels outlandish, selfish, cocky, or entirely irrelevant to the life you are living right now.

You aren't wrong.

What you are seeing is real.

HOW VISION CATALYZES YOUR EFFORT

YOUR GREAT WORK THREAD is an important part of your life's vision, and vision matters a lot. Peter Senge, author of *The Fifth*

Discipline[7], names vision as, "a force in people's hearts, a force of impressive power. Few, if any, forces in human affairs are as powerful as vision." Senge argues that organizations simply can't succeed without clear vision, and I would say the same about Great Work.

Vision acts like a magnet. When you have a powerful, activated vision, you are drawn to it. It pulls at you, convincing you to risk disappointment, failure, and embarrassment for the chance to make it a reality. In this way, a vision generates motivation.

Then, because the magnet is pulling you somewhere specific, your actions accumulate, interact, and reinforce one another to narrow the space between where you are and where you want to be. In short, vision creates momentum.

Without a powerful, activated vision, there is little motivation to do the hard parts of Great Work: having difficult conversations, staying engaged when things fall apart, and putting your work out into the world despite feeling vulnerable. None of this feels worth the risk unless you are headed somewhere you really, deeply want to go.

And even when you *can* dig in and persevere, even your greatest ideas and most courageous actions may dissipate and scatter, leaving you feeling frustrated and disappointed. Think about Chloe: She did a very courageous and difficult thing. She packed up her belongings and moved halfway across the country to take on a new job. She has learned a new organization, a new role, and a new city at the same time. But these efforts weren't in the service of something specific; she wasn't getting any closer to what she really wanted for her work or life. Because of this, despite all that effort, she ended up feeling like she was in the same place as before.

ARE GREAT WORK AND VISION THE SAME THING?

Your Great Work is part of your vision, but your vision is much broader. You can create a vision to guide you toward the house of your dreams, the relationship or family you yearn for, and how you want to feel in your body. Because you are a whole person and balance is important, the vision for your Great Work needs to fit like a puzzle piece inside the larger vision for your life.

ACTIVATING YOUR VISION

TO ENSURE THAT OUR VISION is powerful enough for it to serve as this kind of magnet, we need to activate it. Activating a vision involves feeding it specific details (answering questions such as: Who will be there? What will you do? How will you do it?) and really feeling the emotion of that vision becoming a reality (the pride, excitement, joy, and relief, for example). Infusing your vision with specific, exciting details and honest, deeply felt emotion allows it to take on a life of its own—one so full of possibility that you would do almost anything to bring it into existence.

As you complete the exercise below, go all-in and dream big. Find big feelings—joy over happiness, pride over satisfaction, peace over relief, for example. Feel free to name outcomes that feel completely impossible: Maybe you'll be president, a billionaire, an Olympic gold medalist, or an artist whose art hangs in Le Louvre. We are using these activities to activate your vision, and vision thrives on emotion. It's way more important that you are excited and energized now than that you are eventually proven right.

To that end, don't try to be rational or reasonable:

- Don't worry about logistics. If your vision has you doing stand-up at one a.m. but you are decidedly a morning person, don't let that stop you. Just stay with the excitement and fill in details that feel great.
- Don't argue with yourself about whether something is "even possible." If you are envisioning yourself receiving a Lifetime Achievement Award as the nation's best beekeeper, but you are one hundred percent certain that there is no such award, let it go. The details are there to get you excited, not to show you a crystal ball future! Even if your vision never actually comes true, the point here is to connect with your dream in relation to your Great Work. And who knows—by the time your tenure as a beekeeper is over, there might be just such an award! Maybe you will be its inaugural recipient!

- If you hear your mind pipe up with "You shouldn't do that," or "You should do this instead," shut that voice down. "Shoulds" are clear signs that you've switched from activating your vision to fixating on meeting expectations.

Though I recommend that you complete this activity in the back pages of your *Great Work Journal*, so you can check in with your vision anytime you need a burst of motivation, any notebook will do.

LIFETIME ACHIEVEMENT AWARD

IN ANY NOTEBOOK, FREE WRITE for about twenty minutes on this prompt:

Imagine it's 2050, and you are being honored! Everyone has come to Lincoln Center in appreciation of you and your contributions. This honor could be a famous one, like a Lifetime Achievement Award in entertainment, or something more niche, like a Lifetime Achievement Award in parenting, gardening, standup comedy, fixing bureaucracies, or painting portraits. Let this be a clue to your desires.

Now, imagine yourself settling into the box seats, ready to hear from the people you've helped and reminding you of your accomplishments along the way.

- What are you being honored for?
- How did you contribute? Did you innovate? Revolutionize? Change the face of something?
- How did you get there? Share stories and memories from along the path to greatness.

- Bullet out the accomplishments you earned. Don't be modest; you've done a lot!
- Name relationships you built along the way. Someone you admire is about to say that he or she admires you. Who is it? One of the people you helped is going to say you changed his/her life. Who is it? How did you help? A colleague is telling a riveting story about you. Tell yourself that story.
- At every step: Think big! No, bigger!

When you were activating your Great Work, I hope you went all-in and visualized it in all its manifested glory: "Someday, I want to write the first self-published *New York Times* bestselling book on the Meaning of Life. I will be blown away by five-star reviews on Amazon like this one: 'This book made me aware of my place in the Universe,' and I will, one day, enjoy accepting a Lifetime Achievement Award for 'Changing the Face of Everything.'"

Ahh, that feels *amazing*, doesn't it? That feeling is the very point of vision work! Being emotionally charged about your vision helps you overcome any fear or worry and gives you the courage to move in the right direction. If you continue to feed your Great Work vision high octane emotions, and spend time visualizing, daydreaming, and adding new details as they occur to you, you will benefit from a rare earth magnet (the world's most powerful magnet) sitting right in the center of your Great Work.

Now that you have an idea of what your Great Work is, you are ready to get busy pursuing it!

Or are you?

If the thought of taking on your Great Work feels both exciting *and* a little overwhelming, you may need to clear out some of your commitments and create some time.

We'll dive into this in the next chapter.

CHAPTER THREE

DO LESS—MUCH, MUCH LESS

"People think focus means saying yes to the thing you've got to focus on. But that's not what it means at all. It means saying no to the hundred other good ideas that there are."

Steve Jobs, co-founder of Apple,
and the visionary genius responsible for the iPhone

"I TRIED, BUT I CAN'T just give other people work. I think my company is just more demanding than most," Amber, a management consultant, said during our weekly call. Amber came to me because she wanted to learn how to continue to do well at work, while having time to support her daughter at school. Amber is a single mother of a daughter with autism, and she was frustrated with her school district. She wished that she had the time to join PTA committees and organize school events focused on accessibility and inclusion. But how could she? She was already maxed out at work, working early mornings, late nights, and most weekends.

This particular call was the third such conversation I'd had with Amber in as many weeks. She had been living on the brink of burnout for five years. Recently, that brink had gotten dangerously close to an abyss.

The breaking point came when burnout began to affect her parenting. "I am never going to be a kind, compassionate mother again if I can't get this job under control... let alone spend more time with my daughter or volunteer at her school! How could I possibly do that when I'm barely surviving?"

Consulting is a high-paying job in a competitive job market— two aspects that create the quintessential "golden handcuffs:" that feeling of being trapped by your own good fortune. This can be especially true when you are the sole breadwinner, and you have a daughter with needs that require high-quality health insurance, like Amber.

Few people feel justified complaining about their golden handcuffs, which is one reason burnout runs rampant among these lucky souls. It's also why most of us ignore the signs of exhaustion and burnout until things get really bad.

Things had gotten really bad for Amber, and she sought me out after buying the *Great Work Journal* on Amazon. To create time for Amber to dedicate to her Great Work, our first goal had to be to find a way for her to do much, much less.

Doing less is a difficult first step, because we couldn't *think* our way through it. All the worrying, wondering, and thinking doesn't help; intentions matter very little if our workflow doesn't change.

I CAN'T DO LESS

AMBER WAS STRUGGLING TO TAKE concrete, practical steps to reduce her workflow. She resisted by arguing that she fundamentally *could not* do less. She is not alone! This is very common pushback when people are getting started.

That argument goes like this:

"You don't understand, Amanda. My job is [more demanding, faster paced, more competitive] than most. And unlike a lot of your clients, I don't have a husband/wife with a high-paying job/family money/a trust fund... I really need this job/I *must* succeed/I cannot fail, no matter the cost. Besides, they took a chance on me, and I can't let them down!"

Of course, I can never fully understand another person's struggle, but I have experienced my fair share of a life lived on fumes, as I shared in the first chapter. I've held demanding jobs, and for two years, I ran my coaching company while working in consulting. I have been given some high octane opportunities and felt the consequences of taking them. My husband does have a job, and I'm grateful for that every day, but we don't have family money or a massive nest egg, and my student loans rival the national debt of a small country.

Most of my clients are the same—making it in the world through hard work, grit, and determination. Not a single one of them has the kind of "get-out-of-jail-free card" we sometimes assume everyone else has. There is not a royal or an heiress among them. This doesn't mean that we don't have privilege. Of course we do; everyone does. My point is not to argue that we're living the hard-knock life, but rather that we aren't blessed with the golden goose, either. We're just regular people... probably a lot like you.

While I could try to anticipate and respond to every idea you have about people who can do less, and every reason you could come up with as to why you simply cannot, doing so would actually belabor the very point we are trying to move away from.

Lots of people believe they have to work past the point of exhaustion, meet all expectations, and say "yes" to every good opportunity (no matter how ill-timed or off-point it may be), just like I did.

We believe these things until we don't. And when we decide not to believe these "facts" anymore, and we allow ourselves to make choices that reduce our workload, we discover how much freedom we have actually *always* had.

YOU WILL HAVE TO STOP DOING REAL THINGS IN YOUR REAL LIFE

HAVE YOU EVER TRIED TO park at the airport during rush hour? This is one of the most dangerous things I regularly do. First of all, the path around the airport is like a superhighway from hell: four lanes of traffic filled with cars driven by flustered drivers who are late, worried, and confused. Every ten feet of this particular death trap has both an on-ramp and an off-ramp as cars attempt to navigate five terminals to drop passengers off, pick passengers up, and find the parking lots.

Cars are veering crazily and unexpectedly, crossing four lanes of traffic at the last minute when their drivers realize that the next off-ramp is the *only* way to get to passenger pickup for Terminal C. Then, when they comprehend that what they thought was the off-ramp is actually the on-ramp, and the real off-ramp is on the left, they again veer vertically across traffic, careening into stopped traffic just off the exit.

And can you blame them? If they don't make that exit, they'll have to go all the way around the airport, past all five terminals, one hundred on-ramps, and a thousand dangerous drivers to get to back to where they just were.

Parking at the airport is a great analogy for the way our brain feels when we are working on too many projects at once. In the book *Getting Things Done*, David Allen defines a project as anything that requires at least two action steps to finish. Examples of projects include a client website you're designing, a report you are writing for the end of quarter, tending to your orchid garden, walking your sister's dog, and creating a budget.

When people grasp this concept, they often realize they are working on thirty, forty, or fifty projects all at the same time. They are actively making progress on some, and others are being ignored or procrastinated, but all fifty of them are driving around the brain, causing congestion, shame, and panic. Trying to keep all these cars on the road over-extends our pre-frontal cortex, the part of the brain that suppresses impulses and allows us to be creative problem-solvers. This makes it difficult for us to focus deeply on any one of our projects, leading to less creativity and more errors in our work.

And with this many projects running at once, at least one of them is perpetually about to go off the rails—in response to a missed deadline maybe, or client pressure, or because it's gone way over budget.

Even one crazed project can complicate all the others on the superhighway. Let's say you have an hour between meetings, and you want to take that time to write a cheerful status update email to your favorite client. You want more projects from her! She is easy to collaborate with, a clear communicator, and the work you do together is definitely part of your Great Work. You pull your favorite client car calmly off the highway to write the email.

Just as you settle into your inbox, you see three emails about your problem project. They're all tagged *"Urgent."* Things are on fire in Panic-ville, and you are consumed by putting that fire out for the full hour. Then, at the end of your free time, you realize that you still haven't written that email to your favorite client, thereby taking the energy you planned to give to your favorite project and redirecting it to the worst part of your job.

When you are working on fifty projects, there will *always* be too many things to do and never enough time to do them. When you work on fewer projects, there are fewer things that can hijack your brain. It's that simple.

Which brings us to the point of this analogy:

We have to get some of these projects off the superhighway and out of your brain. Basically, we need your brain to transform out of that rush-hour panic attack and into that "airport at two a.m." vibe: far fewer cars, more freedom to move at your comfortable pace, and a far lower reading on the drama-o-meter.

The sad truth is that this transformation isn't going to happen just because you want it to. In fact, complaining about your workload and generally *intending* to do less is an exercise in futility. If our instinct was to minimize and say "no," we wouldn't be driving around the airport superhighway from hell as we do now. These sincere intentions need to be backed by concrete, practical tactics.

Let me be clear:

In order to do less, you must implement a bunch of the following panic-inducing strategies:

- **Back out of existing commitments.** This is where you say, "I know I said I would do that, but I'm not going to."

- **Put projects, goals, hopes, and dreams in the parking lot.** This takes a project off your radar for now. Maybe the pause lasts only for a weekend, or maybe, it will last for years.
- **Intentionally do B- work.** This involves completing tasks when they are "good enough" to not get you fired *and no better.*
- **Say "NO"** when someone asks you to take on a new task, project, goal, or responsibility.

I know how hard it is to let people down. I have spent many hours worrying myself senseless that I would lose my job, or permanently damage relationships. I tiptoed into doing less, and it was much less dramatic than I had feared. And please trust me that clearing space and making time for what matters will be immediately relieving and deeply gratifying.

After the cold sweat fades, this can feel like winning the lottery.

Let's do this.

THE PROJECT AUDIT

When I do workshops about the Great Work method, we always start with the project audit. This is a quick way to discover how many projects you are trying to keep going at any one time. Here's how to do one for yourself:

1. Make a list of all the categories of projects you are working on. You can have a category like "work projects" or "home improvement project" or "clients."

2. For each category, bullet out the individual projects you have running. I usually have between four and six clients, each one of which is a project. For a category like "run the business" you can have projects like "post on social media," "categorize expenses" or "invoice clients."

3. It's easy to get too granular and end up with *hundreds* of projects. Consider the project "post on social media." You could break that down into "create a content calendar," "write posts," "create images," "schedule posts," and "engage with posts." And, if our goal was to optimize your process, we would do just that. But, when it comes to understanding how many projects you are maintaining at one time, we need bigger chunks. To hit the right level of granularity in your list of projects, think about something that is the right size to delegate.

4. Count how many projects you are managing, and don't be surprised if it's far more than you realized. Don't worry, we're going to get it under control.

BACK OUT OF EXISTING COMMITMENTS

AFTER DISCUSSING THE FULL SCOPE of Amber's over-commitment, I asked her to back out of just one responsibility. She chose coordinating celebrations at work, a time-consuming, monthly obligation where she bought cards and cupcakes to celebrate her colleagues' birthdays and work anniversaries. At first, back when she started at the company, she was happy to do it. It allowed her to meet lots of new people and gave her an excuse to use her company credit card on cupcakes. Win! Five years later, however, the luster had worn off.

"Every month, I feel resentful that I have to stop what I'm doing and handle this random task," Amber said. "There is a new woman on my team who is exactly the right person to do it, and I think she'd be really interested, too."

We discussed her plan: She would run this great idea by her possible replacement. If all went well, Amber would then write an email to the HR woman who provided her with the list of birthdays and anniversaries and hand off the task. Easy!

At our next meeting, however, Amber shared that there "hadn't been time" to discuss the idea with her replacement. Then, at our third meeting, we were back to her generalized litany of overwhelm, and Amber avoided my specific questions about handing off the coordination of celebrations.

Ultimately, with some gentle probing questions and insistent silence, Amber admitted, "I don't know why, but I can't seem to move on it. I've seen her three or four times, and once, she practically asked for the job… but I couldn't bring myself to come out with it."

I wasn't surprised that this seemingly simple handoff was meeting with such resistance. Why would the transfer of a task that didn't need to go through her supervisor and had no impact on her performance review be so difficult?

Because backing out is hard to do. In fact, of the four main strategies that reduce your existing workflow (backing out, putting things on pause, doing B- work, and saying "no"), backing out is *by far* the hardest. It's hard because it involves telling someone else, out loud for all to hear, that you are decisively changing your behavior. It's an assertion of your priorities—a boundary you are erecting that someone else can clearly see.

And that's why we focus on it first.

In our session, I asked Amber whether she secretly enjoyed the task of organizing celebrations.

"No! I mean, I used to enjoy it, but I am truly *over it*."

I asked, "If I could wave a magic wand to remove the task from your plate with no conversations or rigmarole, how would that feel?"

Amber urged me to use my magic wand post-haste.

Unfortunately, I don't have a magic wand, so we did the next best thing. Together, we wrote the email to her colleague asking whether she would be interested in taking over coordinating celebrations. I helped her capture the fun she once experienced doing it, and we framed it as an opportunity. I ignored Amber's desire to "sit with it" and asked her (OK, maybe forced her) to hit "send."

"Oh my God, why am I so sweaty and nervous?" she asked after the deed was done. And then, "Ahhhhhh, I'm so relieved! Even if she says 'no,' which I really don't think she will, I feel so free just from asking!" Amber danced in her seat, eyes shining, new freedom within her grasp.

This is the feeling we are creating in *your* life with this work: FREEDOM.

You get there by asserting your right to choose—to do things, *and stop doing things*—

simply because it's what's right for you.

The first time you back out of a commitment is the worst. The second time is easier, and then, you just might find that you become a freedom-seeking missile, creating time and space for yourself with a focus that rivals a military mission.

Need some help figuring out which things to back out of? Here are a few ideas:

1. **Favors you do for others that they could take care of themselves,** such as picking up snacks for a networking event, finding your mother's plane tickets, or walking your sister's dog. (I mean honestly, your sister is the one who got a dog. Why are you walking it in the middle of the day when you have work to do?)

2. **Optional coordination tasks,** such as a celebrations committee, or your child's Halloween party at school, or organizing the readers at church. These are important jobs, and someone needs to do them. It's time for you to let them!

3. **Client work that annoys you.** You know that client who never pays on time? Or the one who changes her instructions after you've already invested five hours of work? Or the one who treats you like an employee but pays you like an indentured servant? I know it's terrifying to say "goodbye" to paying work, but I also know that a client who drains you takes twice the amount of time he pays for.

4. **Responsibilities at work that you hate,** like the project for which you must navigate Salesforce, which you despise. Or the monthly team meeting you facilitate even though you aren't even on that team any longer. Or let's go for the big kahuna: the huge "opportunity" that has turned out to be nothing but trouble and *so not worth the*

money. Is it time to negotiate a transfer of responsibility? I think it is.

Now, numbers three and four on that list probably raise far more trepidation than the first two, right? That's to be expected. It's one thing to clear the decks of optional projects and volunteer tasks. It's another thing to break up with a client or push back on your job responsibilities.

Eventually, you will need to get serious about your most potent over-commitments, but it's perfectly OK to start small. You can do *a lot* to free up your time and make room for what matters without taking on the biggest, hardest overcommitment in your world.

I just ask that you keep yourself open to bigger ideas that pop into your head: "I should stop working with Stan," or "My annual evaluation is coming up; maybe I should ask to go back to my old team."

Don't discount these ideas. Their day will come.

PANIC BUTTON: EVERYONE WILL HATE ME

To reiterate, backing out of a commitment is hard, because it involves telling other people something that is likely to disappoint them. It's easy to make up stories about how catastrophic it's going to be, which brings on a litany of worry:

"Everyone will hate me."

"I'll lose their trust."

"They'll never give me another opportunity again."

I hear this, and while I agree that it can be excruciating to disappoint someone, here's another truth about human beings:

People are more resilient than we think, and they get used to things quickly.

If you show up strong in your commitment and in service to a larger mission (whether that's the mission of the non-profit you work for, your own mental health, or, in Amber's case, a desire to take good care of her daughter), people will usually work with you.

In my experience, when other people act extremely disappointed, worried, or concerned, it's usually because you seem wishy-washy or uncertain about your commitment. In these instances, they might be wondering if they can avoid a hassle by pressuring you to keep at it. Be careful not to let your own goals and dreams get caught in the net of other people's convenience.

I feel comfortable encouraging you to do this because I'm confident you won't be a rash asshole—or, as I like to call it, a rash-hole. Rash-holes are people who overcommit, and then, *at the last minute,* back out of things with little to no consideration for the mess they are leaving for others to clean up.

Please don't do be a rash-hole unless you absolutely must—like to avoid a bona fide mental health crisis, or because your physical health is at stake, or your loved ones are in danger. Instead of wreaking chaos on your collaborators, realize that walking back your commitments takes time and consideration. Then, work to respectfully hand them off or shut things down.

When Amber got the email from her colleague agreeing to take over celebrations, she was two weeks away from the company's monthly get-together. Amber used it as an opportunity to show her colleague *how* to do the work by doing the coordination together. Then, the following month, she made herself available for questions and left the responsibility in the capable hands of her colleague. Amber was not a rash-hole, and you won't be either, when you back out of a commitment responsibly.

All that said, you must also be OK with disappointing other people. When Amber told her HR contact that she was handing off the celebrations responsibility to her colleague, the HR representative was disappointed and a little bit short. She enjoyed working with Amber and didn't want something easy to become difficult. Amber was momentarily upset and worried that she had "ruined everything."

Of course, she hadn't.

It was a small frustration for the HR representative, and it passed quickly. But even if your collaborator is *very disappointed*, and it's going to be *almost impossible* for her to replace you, *it's still worth it*. Ultimately, we must realize that while it's appropriate to be considerate about the inconvenience we cause, it's not appropriate to let another person's frustration derail us from doing our Great Work and enjoying our lives. In Amber's case, it was worth the discomfort to enjoy her job again and create space to take care of her daughter.

In short, people will get used to things quickly.

They *will* find another way.

PUT PROJECTS, GOALS, HOPES, AND DREAMS IN THE PARKING LOT

You can't, nor do you want to, back out of everything. And yet, projects that you won't let go of entirely still need a way to be removed from your active involvement, at least for a while.

These things aren't being eliminated from your life! You are just putting them out of your mind for a few days, weeks, months, or maybe years.

These might be things you care about but just can't fit in right now, like doing yoga, growing irises, writing a book, learning to sew, reading the collected works of Shakespeare, or mending a frayed relationship with your brother.

They might be less urgent aspects of your job description, like reaching out to new partnership organizations, upgrading the database, or finding a new vendor for your supplies.

Or it could be things that you are entirely expected to do—by everyone, *including yourself*—and to violate that expectation is way too painful and overwhelming to consider. These might be tasks like helping your mother move, talking to your sister about her divorce, or nurturing your child's love of animals.

All these things are valid, important, and maybe even critical. Doing them shows that you are kind, caring, dedicated, thorough, steady, and reliable.

And doing all of them at the same time is making your life hell.

It's time to intentionally park some of these projects.

- You can park them in short-term parking by putting them out of your mind for a few hours, a weekend, a week, or a month.
- You can put them in medium-term parking and plan to return to them in two to nine months.
- Or you can put them in long-term parking and plan to return to them "eventually."

Projects that you are actively monitoring but on which you aren't making any progress are a big source of shame and worry. Putting those projects in the parking lot instead allows you to acknowledge and accept that *for now* things will have to stay as they are.

SHORT-TERM PARKING: A BRIEF HIATUS

I TRIED THIS FOR THE first time when I was a freshman in college. My father was struggling with his addictions and had left his home. He was known to be staying in a heroin den just outside of Detroit. My grandmother called me in a panic several times, asking me to intervene.

Even now, I'm not sure what she expected me to do from 500 miles away. I suspect she mostly didn't want to be alone with her fear. Either way, I was consumed by worry. I hadn't experienced a heroin den so I had nothing to go on. And yet, for about a week straight I made myself sick wondering what it might be like.

This whole drama was playing out against the backdrop of my very first semester in college. It was finals week, just before the holidays. I remember sitting on my top bunk in my freshman dorm, staring at the pile of work I needed to do finish out my semester. *I won't be able to focus on this if I'm consumed by worry for my dad. Just for the next few days, I'll put it out of my mind. I will refuse to think about it until after finals. Then, I'll drive up and see what I can do.*

Without knowing it, I drove my worry into short-term parking. I wasn't callously deciding my father's turmoil didn't matter. But I also wasn't going to let his choices derail my life in the short term. It worked well. I got a break from the all-consuming worry, and I finished my final projects. Then, I called my grandmother. It turns out that while I was busy finishing my finals, my father had returned home.

Short-term parking is great for things that are of ongoing concern, but *in the short term,* they are also distractions. Intentionally removing things from your radar can help you focus more deeply, make quicker progress on your highest-leverage projects, and provide yourself some relief.

It's not always painful things that you want to put in short-term parking. You may have a project that you *love* working on—redecorating your home, for example, or collaborating with a friend to plan an event—yet, for a week or two, you just need it to disappear. You can't do what you need to do *and* keep that passion project going. So, rather than trying to keep a little sliver of your brain focused on it, decide to take a few weeks off from it completely. If you are worried that you'll lose track of it, add a reminder to your calendar to follow up later. Then, park the project.

These days, I'm better at prioritizing my projects, and I use short-term parking mostly as a means of setting up boundaries that allow me to be present in the moment. In the evenings, before I end my workday and pick up my kids, I consciously put all my work into short-term parking. *I'm not going to think about this until tomorrow morning. Whatever happens between now and nine a.m. is going to happen, and I don't need to keep an eye on it.* And then, I turn my brain entirely to family life. This is a surprisingly effective strategy! I know I am making a choice and that I could wake up the following morning to a dumpster fire in my inbox. I accept that risk, because being focused exclusively on my family is important to me.

MEDIUM-TERM PARKING: PRIORITIZING YOUR MOST IMPORTANT PROJECTS

MEDIUM-TERM PARKING IS FOR PROJECTS that are great ideas, very good next steps, and/or powerful objectives… but it's *just not the time* for them.

If you are anything like me, you have *a lot* of ideas. I have ideas for revisions to my university psychology courses, for programs and online courses I could create in my business, books I could write, events I could host, people I could collaborate with. On and on it goes. If I moved on every idea I have, I would never sleep, and misery would be my default mode. I know, because before I became serious about using the tactics in this chapter, that *was* my life.

These days, almost all my great ideas initially go into medium-term parking. They sit there at least until I start a new round of 90-day goals. I used to think if I didn't move quickly on an idea, I would miss out on something critical. FOMO (fear of missing out) is real. I was always trying to write a blog, get a new client, launch a new online course, and learn to speak French all at the same time. Some of these projects got done, but I was so drained by the constant multi-tasking that I didn't enjoy doing them.

In 2018, I created an online mindset course called *Success Is an Inside Job*. I re-watched some of the videos the other day to find a resource I wanted to send to a client, and I realized: I really like it! But my memory of making it is of grinding away, staying up late to prepare videos for the editor while trying to meet with *all my clients* ahead of a two-week vacation. It was such a slog! I regret that something I created and really appreciate now was such a drain at the time. These days, I realize doing *a lot* is much less important than enjoying what I'm doing.

Medium-term parking has another benefit. Projects that are truly great grow in energy and juice over time, and when I'm ready to start a new project, I'm excited and motivated to get going. Some projects that sound great at the outset lose their momentum and fade into oblivion within just a few weeks. For this reason, it's very savvy to give projects some room to breathe; the ones that are great will stick, while the ones that are destined for oblivion don't waste our precious time.

LONG-TERM PARKING: KEEPING OUR DREAMS SAFE WHILE WE DO OTHER THINGS

LONG-TERM PARKING HOLDS ALL THE great ideas that still have some juice, but just aren't aligned with what we're hoping to accomplish right now. And yes, some projects remain in long-term parking for a *long time*. For example, someday I really, really want to learn to play the piano and speak fluent French. I'd like to hike the Appalachian trail and bike across the country. And I'd like to be a part of creating a children's television show. None of these things are happening right now in any serious way.

The ideas in long-term parking are a source of inspiration. They push me to watch movies in French, read books about long-term hikers, and listen to beautiful piano music. And maybe that's all they'll ever do. That's OK. (Except for that children's television show. That's gonna happen. I just know it.)

INTENTIONALLY DO B- WORK

OK, NOW THAT WE'VE GOTTEN as much as we can off your plate—either by backing out or by putting things in the parking lot—it's time to minimize the impact of some of your lower-leverage work.

Remember how your work was graded in school? When you turned in a paper and got an A+, you felt so good. So productive. So *accomplished*. Right?

The writing was on the wall: All work should be done to the best of your ability. All work should be improved until it is perfect, because that's how you meet your potential and please the people who matter.

Well, my friends, this is one of the ways in which the education system lied to you. The point of your life is not to *do a lot of things perfectly*, but to *do Great Work*.

If you are going to create the space for Great Work, you're going to have to de-program yourself. It's true that some work— your most creative, interpersonal, and innovative work (ahem, the Great kind)—should be done to the best of your ability. And some work should be done to a level of good enough *and no more*. From here forward, we'll refer to the "good enough" work as "B- work."

Yes, I am fully encouraging you to do *average* work. And I don't mean "average for you," if you are someone accustomed to earning a 3.5 or above GPA. I'm talking average for the rest of us; which is to say, not very good. Lagging. Vague. B- work could definitely be better, but you *choose* to leave it at "good enough."

It's not that you don't *do* the work; it's that you do the work in a lackluster way, intentionally. Very specifically, I am saying to voluntarily and knowingly do some of your work in such a way that someone, like your boss, might think, "That's not great. It could have been better." And knowing this, you will *continue* to do the task in a sub-par manner.

Of course, I'm not suggesting that you do *all* of your work as B- work. You must still deliver the highest quality of work possible on the things that matter. What I *am* saying is that every single person on the planet has some work that requires nothing other than that it get done. If you do *that* work with less effort, you can free up a ton of your time.

Great candidates for B- work include tasks that support the real work, such as writing emails, reporting and documenta-tion, participating in meetings, or keeping someone in the loop. Of course, what B- work actually looks like depends entirely upon your industry, company, and workflow. In regulation-heavy industries, reporting matters more than the client-facing meetings themselves. In other industries, the reports are read by no one and should be competently accomplished but no more.

Discovering which tasks can be done as B- work requires experimentation and can, every now and then, backfire in a minor way. That's OK. We are so committed to freeing up our time that it's worth it. We are willing to put in the effort, make mistakes, and discover what works through trial and error.

When I worked in consulting, I was met with a daily emailpalooza that consumed probably 25-35 percent of my time. While some of the emails were important, the vast majority were from people chiming in or following up or scheduling. I started out bringing my best self to every email. I was careful to be one of the first to chime in on emails seeking feedback. I wrote readable and interesting summaries of meetings and followed up on scheduling with all the grace of a duchess. Some of that changed when I realized that many of these emails would lose nothing when done with B- work. I asked myself which of these emails really mattered versus which ones were lost work that no one cared about. Based on my answer, I made the following adjustments to my workflow:

1. **I stopped responding immediately.** Realizing that the emails asking everyone to chime in were usually either serving as a poll or an attempt to cover off with stakeholders, I decided to sit on them. Rather than jumping right in and trying to prove my worth, I'd wait for a few hours and wait to see what others had to say. Then, when someone said exactly what I would have said (as someone *always* did), I'd chime in with an "I agree with Pete!" Or, if I cared about the issue at hand and it seemed that the request for feedback was genuine, I would add something substantive to the existing conversation: "I agree with Pete and wonder whether we should also bring Jell-O." (Now you're wondering what kind of meetings we had at this company, aren't you?)

2. **I implemented an online scheduler.** I started sending calendar scheduling links (such as one would get through a service like Calendly, or Acuity): "Here's a link to my

calendar. Time are filling up quickly next week, so hop on and grab something that works for you." I found it to be so much more actionable than playing the world's worst game of tag: "Here are four more times that might work for you." Reply: "Those don't work for me. What about these?" And round and round you go.

3. **I discovered the voice memo.** Often, we are over-delivering beyond what anyone needs or wants. When I asked my colleagues what they needed from our post-meeting check-in emails, we realized that dictating voice memos as I was leaving the meeting—instead of writing summaries—was better for everyone. It was as much of a relief for my email-inundated co-workers as it was for me.

You may be wondering, did every single experiment with B- work go unnoticed? No. I remember one experiment where I did not send an email reminder for a meeting, and half the attendees didn't show. That mattered.

Another time, I sent a small, measly, insignificant (to me) report to a client without running it past my boss beforehand. He responded with a very polite-yet-irritated email that said: "I had planned to add the budget breakdown when you sent it. Now, I have to send it separately." We live and learn.

Some people care about things you don't care about.

Fine.

Give them what they want.

But if you give B- work a shot, I think you'll be surprised by how much A+ effort is getting lost to the ether of "no one cares."

PANIC BUTTON: HAVE YOU NO STANDARDS?

When I introduced Amber to the concept of intentionally doing B- work, she had a strong, negative, fear-based reaction. "That might work in some industries, but in consulting, everything matters! This would get me fired."

People in every industry believe that while other people have it easier, their specific circumstances make for a highly specialized set of non-negotiables that render ease and intention impossible. People who work in finance point to rules and regulations, saying, "People's retirements are at stake!" People in education, healthcare, and social services say, "People's lives are at stake!" People in business for themselves might feel it most of all, declaring, "My whole life is at stake!"

And these things are true—the stakes are high in our work. And high stakes, by their nature, are stressful and need to be taken seriously.

Taking the high stakes of your work—*and your life*—seriously is exactly what I'm asking you to do by encouraging B- work. I am not blithely suggesting you phone it in so you can take advantage of loopholes and other peoples' effort. I'm asking you, instead, to take a hard look at two very serious truths:

1. **You are already doing B- work.** There are places where things are falling through the cracks, getting dashed off at the last second, and being unfairly pushed off onto others. But you aren't in control of it. You aren't *choosing* to direct your B- effort on things that don't matter, take a lot of time, and aren't critical. Instead, you are being

haphazard; sometimes that B- effort is being deployed to things that matter the most, need more time than you give them, and are critical to your advancement, potential, and Great Work.

2. **If you don't make time for what matters, you'll never get to it.** All the tips in this chapter are designed to *change* your default behavior. That's not a natural or easy thing to do. They require that you be more strategic, more honest about your time, and more focused on what will get you closer to what you want.

Even if all you want in this life is to do your existing job better, doing less of what doesn't matter will serve you well. But if you want to get the opportunity to join high-visibility teams, write a book, go on international adventures, get a promotion, or any of the other exciting things you see others do with envy in your heart (a classic indicator that it's part of your Great Work), it's especially important that you are strategic and intentional about how you spend your time.

The things that matter take more time. So, if you want to do them, you need to make some time for them.

If backing out of a commitment is something that sounds like a good idea but is hard for you to execute, doing B- work is the opposite. It sounds like a terrible idea, I know. But I assure you, when you start to execute it, it is the BEST. THING. EVER. You will realize how much effort you can eliminate from the margins without it ever impacting your work negatively. You will love being more efficient, delivering on your high-stakes work with less resentment. And, best of all, you will have *more time*. All by itself, this can be life-changing.

NOW THAT YOU'VE CLEARED THE SPACE, *SAY "NO"*

You've done it; you've backed out of some projects, put a bunch in the parking lot, and strategically implemented B- work that no one has noticed. You feel great! You have time! Space! And your Great Work has begun to get some traction.

Then, someone asks you to do something. Maybe it's a really good opportunity. Not exactly aligned with your goals, but a good idea in a vacuum. Or perhaps someone needs help, and it's pulling on your heart strings. Or, more subversively, perhaps the ask is coming through back-channel guilt, insinuating that if you don't help, you're a jerk who only cares about yourself.

This is a critical moment.

I see you looking at your "free time" and thinking, "Well, I could help them now that I'm no longer walking my sister's dog four times a day."

I need you to resist this urge.

I want you to open your mouth and say, "No."

You didn't do all this clearing to fill it back up with other people's agenda items. You cleared this space so you can figure out how to do the things that matter to *you*, to make time, space, headspace, and room in your calendar to learn how to do your Great Work while taking care of your health and happiness! To double down on your full potential. To spark greatness, and nurture it into a raging fire that brings warmth to thousands.

Do not go backwards.

Stay strong.

Saying "No" is an ongoing practice. There is always another opportunity, another favor, and another project that you'll need to resist. The *Great Work Journal* will support you in this effort, too.

Every week and every day, as you plan, you will be asked: What will you say "NO" to this week? What will you say "NO" to today? Setting boundaries ahead of time is a powerful way to hold your own against the onslaught of requests that will almost certainly come your way. This daily recommitment to protecting your time and avoiding overcommitment is one of the best things about the journal.

GOOD THINGS COME FROM DOING LESS

I WORKED WITH AMBER FOR about six months. She backed out of projects, created some solid B- work, put all her extra ideas into their proper parking space, and was ready, finally, to spend time with her daughter. She had a then seven-year-old daughter, and her dream was to finish at six every day and sneak away early once a week to spend an afternoon with her.

Then, her boss offered her a promotion (this happens a lot, by the way—as soon as you are in control of your life and time, people will realize how much more you can do! Suddenly, when you aren't in chaos from doing too much, people see your potential, feel your power, and want you to be involved. It's a good thing).

Amber was torn. She was a single mother, and a promotion would mean more money… but she had just gotten to a place where she was finally feeling better: less burnt out, more emotionally available at home, and enjoying her work again.

With the courage of her commitment in full view, Amber turned down the promotion. She cried in disappointment, fully knowing that it was the best thing for her and her daughter. She worried that she had just killed her career, lost her last chance to manage a bigger team, and disappointed her boss so completely that she would eventually lose her job.

I checked in with her recently, and none of those things happened. In fact, in the intervening couple of years, her boss offered her a better, more aligned promotion, which she took. Now, she's currently in the running for a vice-president role. Her boss, far from being disappointed, told her that she appreciated that she could count on Amber to take on work she could do and be honest about work that was outside of scope or lower priority.

In short, she trusted Amber to be in charge of her time, not at the mercy of it. And this made her a *more valuable employee*, not a disappointment. And, importantly, Amber helped to organize an Abilities Fair at her daughter's school, which is now an annual affair. Win-win.

OK, BUT WHAT IF I DON'T SAY "NO?"

No MATTER HOW SUCCESSFUL YOU are at clearing your schedule and doing less, don't think that this is a one-and-done kind of deal. Not by a long shot! In fact, I think I could sum up the past twenty-five years of my professional career as a repeating pattern of "do too much, get overwhelmed, pull back." Repeat. Around and around. As a person with a lot of ideas and a lot of enthusiasm, I am my own worst enemy. I get a lot of opportunities, and I take too many of them.

And then there I am, working on the weekend, checking email when I wake up at three a.m., and spending most of my time putting out fires.

Basically, I am always right here, in this cycle.

When I realize that I *yet again* find myself overwhelmed and overcommitted, racing around the airport with too many cars changing lanes while things spin out of control, I know what to do:

1. Back out.
2. Park some projects.
3. Do B- work.
4. Recommit to saying "No"
5. Get back to what matters.

This is a *process*. It's not something you can just "set and forget." So be kind to yourself, and assume that you will be using these skills again and again. The good news is that now that you've figured out what you want, you are motivated to do this difficult work. You'll find your way, because you are doing it for your daughter, like Amber. Or for your world-changing business, or jaw-dropping art, or innovation that changes everything.

You'll do it for your Great Work.

CHAPTER FOUR

HOW TO MAKE YOUR GREAT WORK A REALITY

"It's a terrible thing, I think, to wait until you're ready.
I have this feeling now that actually no one is ever ready
to do anything. There is almost no such thing as 'ready.'
There is only now. And you may as well do it now.
Generally speaking, now is as good a time as any."

*Hugh Laurie, Golden Globe winning actor from
the long-running television show,* House MD

ANNA IS A WOMAN ON a mission. At least, that's how she feels
when she's talking about her dream of starting a nonprofit
organization that provides art therapy for veterans. She began
working at the Department of Veterans Affairs (VA) as a therapy
provider when she was in her late 20s and discovered how
powerful expressive art therapy was when used by veterans
healing from the shock and trauma of war.

"It connects them back to a part of themselves that got
suppressed during their active duty. It's like watching a whole

new version of themselves emerge from our work together. When art therapy works, it *works*," she said. While Anna continued to work at the VA full time, she wanted to lay groundwork for her nonprofit.

Anna's vision for her Great Work is rock solid. She has no problem getting excited about the opportunities that she could create for veterans and for herself. "What I really want is to make art therapy free for veterans. Any veteran, no matter when or where they did their service, should be able to explore that experience through art. And I want to have an art gallery full of artwork from veterans, because I think if people see the art, they'll more deeply understand the sacrifice our soldiers are making. And I would love to shape the national conversation about war, service, honor, and what it means to support our veterans when they come home."

Yet, despite her outright enthusiasm and deep content knowledge, Anna was not making progress on her dream. "It's reached the point where I'm almost embarrassed to talk about it with my family and friends. They ask me how it's going, and I just shrink."

"I don't know what my problem is," she continued. "I know I'm a hard worker—I work *all the time*—and I get so excited by the idea of creating my nonprofit. Why have I done so little? Every now and then I search the internet looking for names of veterans' groups to connect with… but that's it. That's everything I've done. In a *year*."

This is very common. We hit on our great idea, get excited about it, and then… nothing really happens. Everything that comes to mind either feels too small to make a difference or so large it's paralyzing. It's no wonder we give up and decide to think about it tomorrow. Confusing vision with goals is one of the most common sources of frustration when people are trying to make progress on their Great Work. That confusion is frustrating *by its nature.* Let's say Anna has an hour to work on her nonprofit after a long day at the VA. How could she use one hour to "shape the national conversation?" She can't.

Another common source of frustration is when we to try to chip away at something before we have a functional vision for it. In Chapter 2, we heard from Chloe who was busy changing jobs, moving cities, and learning new roles, and was left feeling like she was spinning her wheels. To solve both problems, we need to first clarify the nature of our ideas and then align our time to those ideas in the right way, depending on the type of idea it is.

WHAT KIND OF IDEA DO YOU HAVE?

AT THE CORE OF MUCH of this frustration is a lack of clarity about *ideas.* A vision is an idea, and so is a goal. So is a task, and a to-do. If you are anything like Anna, or me, or 98 percent of my clients, you are awash in ideas. Ideas come in the shower, while you are walking the dog, doing morning pages, or simply "out of nowhere." And this is before we even get to the goals, tasks, and to-dos that come rolling out of meetings, conversations, and emails!

As the ideas flow in, you've likely noticed that they vary quite a lot.

Some will be small, on the level of: "Maybe Matt could help with my budget." Some may be much larger, like, "I want to write a bestselling book."

These are clearly not the same *kind* of ideas, right?

I like to categorize ideas into five different levels, visualized as an upside-down triangle:

- Level 1: A **catalyzing vision** you hope to achieve "someday."
- Level 2: An **accessible aspiration** you plan to achieve in the next year or two.
- Level 3: A **90-day goal**, toward which you are actively striving, that you know will take weeks, but not years.
- Level 4: A **weekly task** you will do, appropriately, this week.
- Level 5: A **to-do** you've got on your list for today.

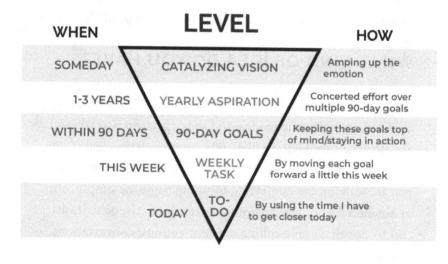

It's helpful to understand how your ideas fit into this structure, because the best way to align your time to an idea depends on its level. If your idea is something you can do today, such as "Ask Matt for help," then the best thing you can do is put it on a to-do list or in the daily pages of the *Great Work Journal*, and then do it.

If your idea is on the level of a catalyzing vision, like Anna's world-changing non-profit, then you need to do two things: First, activate it (as discussed in Chapter 2), and then translate your vision into the lower levels of the triangle, so you can take concrete action.

THE ACCESSIBLE ASPIRATION

FOR ANNA TO MOVE OUT of paralysis and into action, her first step was to translate her vision into an accessible aspiration. Accessible aspirations are aptly named. They must feel accessible and doable, but still kind of far away. They will take multiple 90-day goal cycles and a lot of figuring out. Unlike a vision, which has a nebulous "someday" feeling, accessible aspirations feel tied to the real calendar. Usually, I think of these as ideas as "on tap" in the next one or two years.

Anna realized that if she was going to build a successful nonprofit, she needed to conquer fundraising. She decided to start by trying to fund a pilot program in about a year. This aspiration begins to put Anna into the flow of concrete work. It helps to her realize that she's going to need to make connections, hone her pitch, and find opportunities to collaborate. But even an accessible aspiration can be overwhelming when you are trying to decide what to do (and what *not* to do) in the next three months. For this, we need to head down into the next level: 90-day goals!

WHY SET 90-DAY GOALS

YOU MAY HAVE NOTICED THAT 90-day goals are all the rage. If you are somewhat of a rebel (I see you!), you probably want to know why before you blindly follow along.

Let's first acknowledge that ninety days is actually pretty arbitrary. You could set a ten-week goal, and that would be equally fine. Or a four-month goal, which is what I recommend for people who are still in school—if you are tied to semesters, just go with it!

Nonetheless, I like 90-day goals because:

- They give us four chances each year to make things happen. With four cycles, we can do a lot.
- If you follow the quarters of the fiscal year (starting your goals in January, April, July, and October), it makes you feel like you are part of something bigger. You can start saying things like "Q2 goals" and bemoan the "end of the quarter" along with everyone else. This is a powerful piece of identity-building, if part of your Great Work is building a business.
- With 90-day goals, you can roughly follow the seasons. If you live in a seasonal place, your life probably feels significantly different in January than it does in July. I'm not making a claim that January or June is more productive, because that depends on you and the weather in your part of the world. Rather, I'm noting that some goals will feel more appropriate and accessible based on the time of year. 90-day goals allow for that.
- We can generally predict what we will be doing in the next ninety days in a way we can't when we look any further into the future[8]. For example, could you have a dinner with a friend on the second Tuesday in three months? How about five? Go to your calendar and try to answer that question. Do you notice a difference?

- The 90-day timeframe is long enough that you *will definitely* want to quit. But you won't! At least not until your ninety days are up. Part of what we are doing here is re-establishing trust with ourselves that we will stay with our goals long enough to accomplish something significant. You can't do that with a goal so short that you never want to quit!

LEVELS DEPEND ON EXPERIENCE

It's important to note that if Anna were starting her third nonprofit, her vision for a nonprofit would likely be an accessible aspiration. Since Anna had *never* started a nonprofit but had spent her entire career in government, her big idea was at the level of catalyzing vision.

That doesn't mean it will stay there for long! It could be that with the right help, a few favors, and a little visibility, her vision could quickly become an accessible aspiration or even a ninety-day goal. But it wouldn't have helped for her to expect her grand idea to operate like an accessible aspiration or 90-day goal right away, *because that's not where she was at*. Having overly high expectations can cause a lot of shame and negative self-talk, which shut down progress.

HOW TO PICK YOUR GOALS: THE 3-S GOAL STRUCTURE

TAKING ON MORE THAN THREE goals related to Great Work at one time makes most people feel overwhelmed and stretched in every direction. And yet, despite how much better it feels to be focused, this three-goal ideal is *very difficult* for some people! As we discussed in Chapter 3, some of us are concurrently pursuing *dozens* of goals and projects, and the idea of narrowing to three feels almost illicit. Also in Chapter 3, we talked through how to say "no," back out, and park some of your projects. If you haven't taken that work to heart, choosing only three goals may feel very challenging. It might help to go back and take another look at your project audit, and move a few more things off the radar.

Of the three, only one of these goals is a stretch goal. The other two goals are a support goal and a sanity goal, which together provide a solid foundation from which to achieve your stretch goal.

AT THE HEART OF YOUR GREAT WORK: THE STRETCH GOAL

YOUR STRETCH GOAL IS THE beating heart of your Great Work. It usually requires research, help-seeking, the learning of new skills, and a whole lot of failure. Your stretch goal will also force you to overcome hurry, worry, guilt, overwhelm, hustle, and perfectionism. This is the piece you've chosen to get your hands dirty with; you know you'll make mistakes; and you are confident that on the other side of those mistakes is victorious, glorious *progress*.

In short, stretch goals require the most willpower.

Willpower is our ability to focus on things when we don't want to and to do complex tasks when we want to do easy things instead. Willpower is a limited resource in humans[9], because it's housed in the newest (in terms of evolution) part of our brain— the prefrontal cortex. The prefrontal cortex is responsible for helping us make hard decisions, focus on difficult tasks, and suppress our urge to give up.

The interesting thing about your prefrontal cortex is that it gets tired. Other parts of your brain don't; your limbic system, for example, doesn't ever get tired of helping you breathe.

The prefrontal cortex, on the other hand, runs out of juice. Think about it: By the end of the day, you are much more likely to eat a whole box of cookies, yell at one of the lucky people who live with you, and cry. Right? You're also much more likely to put off making hard decisions and avoid new and novel problems like the plague. This is what it looks like when your prefrontal cortex has lost its mojo.

And this is why I recommend having only *one* stretch goal. These taxing goals drain our limited willpower and make us tired. Great Work is worth the drain, obviously, but doing too many difficult projects at once leads to burnout, unhappiness, and sacrifice. That's against the rules in this book! One stretch goal is enough.

Anna decided that in the next 90 days she would have at least twelve conversations with fundraisers, executive directors, and program leaders at veterans-focused non-profits. That's roughly one conversation a week. She called it her "listening tour," because she didn't want the pressure of pretending to be an expert.

"I'm excited to hear about their experience of fundraising and building awareness, and I'm forcing myself to acknowledge that I'm a novice who is there to learn."

EXPLORING YOUR GOALS

When setting 90-day goals, it's helpful to spend some time exploring your goal before you dive in. This will help you figure out how to begin, and provide you with a list of ideas for when you need a new strategy. It will also provide handy reminders for when you feel like giving up. The *Great Work Journal* has a page dedicated to these questions for each goal, but you can also ask yourself these same questions in any notebook.

◎ MY STRETCH GOAL FOR THE NEXT 90 DAYS IS:

Have 12 conversations with fundraisers, executive directors, and program leaders at veterans-focused non-profits

♥ Why does this goal matter to me?

I want to be known in this community, and I don't want to try to learn everything on my own.

What obstacles are likely to get in my way?	How will I overcome this obstacle?
I don't know 12 people!	*Trust that people will connect you. You just need somewhere to start.*
I'm so tired already... how do i find time for all this networking?	*I need to make my sanity goal to go to bed on time. And I can book some of these for lunch time.*
What if they think I'm inept and naive?	*Call it a listening tour so you are being upfront about just getting started.*

💧 What resources do I have to help me achieve this goal?
Who can I ask for help?

My contact at Wounded Warrior, ask Andrew's Dad for help. I can also use the attendee list from the conference I went to this summer.

⚡ Brainstorm small steps that you can take right away. Whenever you get stuck, you can return to this list and begin again. Don't worry if you don't fill every line—as ideas occur to you over the next 90 days, you can add them to the list.

- ○ *Find the name of the guy at Wounded Warrior and send him an email.*
- ○
- ○
- ○
- ○
- ○

MAKING THE DREAM POSSIBLE: THE SUPPORT GOAL

THE NEXT GOAL IN THE 3-S Goal Structure is the support goal. The support goal is designed to make your stretch goal easier, more accomplishable, and, in some cases, possible. A support goal might provide stability in a related area or address an issue that tends to arise at inconvenient times. Examples might include tracking your finances better, posting on social media more regularly (if building a social platform for your business is important), or automating your calendar scheduling and reminders.

Support goals are often (though not always) goals that focus on process instead of projects. While stretch goals often have a clear accomplishment associated with them (write the book, close the deal, file the incorporation paperwork), support goals often focus on getting better at doing something (exercise more often, keep better records, get better sleep)[10]. Process goals are critical because these habits form the foundation of our lives, but they can feel nebulous. You can *always* get better sleep, because you are always going to need to sleep, and your sleep is never perfect. This can make process goals feel less satisfying because they are never done. It helps to give your process goal a clear finish line for the sake of your 90-day goals, so you can measure your progress. Instead of "get better sleep," choose "get to bed by ten p.m. at least four nights a week." Instead of "keep better records," choose "file all claims within two weeks."

Anna's 90-day support goal was to network more regularly. She was regularly invited to conferences and events both at the

VA and in the larger DC region, but was so tired from work that she skipped most of them. Her support goal, then, was to change her ways and attend more of these opportunities to network. Her support goal intersected with her stretch goal directly:

"If I go to one of these networking events at least every two weeks, I should meet enough people to find the twelve conversations for my listening tour."

KEEPING YOU RESILIENT: THE SANITY GOAL

THE FINAL GOAL IN THE 3-S Goal Structure is the sanity goal. This goal focuses on something that makes you feel grounded, resourced, and resilient. Resilience is the ability to bounce back, recover from disappointment, and continue despite failure. It's related to willpower (in the sense that we are more resilient earlier in the day), and to vision (since vision creates the motivation that keeps us invested when things feel hard).

The nature of Great Work requires you to learn new things and put yourself out in the world: two things that activate all the drama and drain your willpower. The sanity goal *is critical* to the success of your stretch and support goals, because it keeps you resilient enough stay at it when it get hard.

Chapter 5 outlines habits and choices that might make good sanity goals. For now, though, just make sure you are choosing something that would make you feel good *even before you accomplish it*. For example, if you choose going to yoga three times a week, make sure that going to yoga even just once feels pretty great. The point of this goal is to give you the gift of groundedness, support, and strengths, right away and all along the way.

You might have already guessed Anna's sanity goal, based on her support goal. She was staying up late and getting up early trying to keep everything going. Her sanity goal, then, was to be better rested, so she could have the energy to make good connections while networking. When Anna went through the activities we did in the last chapter—putting things on pause and backing out of any unnecessary commitments—she found some time.

"I need to use some of that time to get more sleep!" she said. "I'm going to figure out what it takes to go to bed by ten every night."

90-DAY GOAL FAQ:

Do We Only Ever Work on Our Three Goals?

My hope for you is that as time goes on, more of your time will be dedicated to what matters the most to you. I've managed to align about 50-60 percent of my time to my Great Work. I'm coaching, teaching, writing, and speaking more and more every week, and it feels good.

Of course, that means that 40-50 percent of my time is still tied up in "the rest of it." I'm writing emails, doing paperwork, grading, doing observations, and serving on committees.

This is OK, because all work—no matter how great—requires that we do the boring parts, too. Plus, I'm committed to doing my Great Work before I have time and before I'm ready. If I was waiting until I could focus on it exclusively, I'd be waiting forever.

I Can't Decide on My 90-Day Goals! What Should I Do?

After years of setting 90-day goals, I'm here to tell you: Choosing good 90-day goals takes *practice*.

First, there's the problem of the size of the goal. Inevitably, as we get started setting 90-day goals, we will choose some that are wayyyy too big (I'll write and publish my book!) and some that are wayyyy too small for ninety days (I'll finally schedule an appointment with the functional medicine doctor!). We want goals that take at least multiple weeks of strong effort, and sometimes, consistent effort across all ninety days.

Don't worry if you find yourself over- or underwhelmed by your goals at first. You will get started on the big ones, blow through the little ones, and eventually discover how to create perfect, Goldilocks-sized goals.

Then, there's the problem of setting a goal that can, objectively, be accomplished. Very often, people set goals like "Get better at yoga." While I know that they do, in fact, want to get better at yoga, these kinds of goals are difficult to track. How would they know that they have accomplished it? We can always get even better!

It's easy to feel endlessly behind when your goal is open-ended. We are looking for concrete goals, so we know when we've done it. "Figure out how to do a headstand" is better. And so is, "Figure out how to go to yoga three times a week." In both cases, you will know whether you have accomplished them.

As is true for all things in this book, your goal is to get started, not to do it perfectly. If that means you are working with imperfect and incomplete goals, so be it! It's more important that you get into the habit of setting and pursuing 90-day goals; your skill level will improve exactly as quickly as it needs to.

Are We Setting SMART Goals?

What you're reading may remind you of SMART goals: goals that are Specific, Measurable, Attainable, Relevant, and Time-bound. I've this up to ensure that your goals are SMART without the analysis paralysis that tends go with *trying to set* a SMART goal.

For the goal nerds out there, here's the breakdown:

- The goals are Specific and Measurable, so we know when we have accomplished them.
- They are Attainable, because they align to the 3-S Goal Structure, and tied to an attainable aspiration, which keeps things contained.
- They are relevant because they connect to your Great Work and vision.
- And they are time-bound by ninety days.

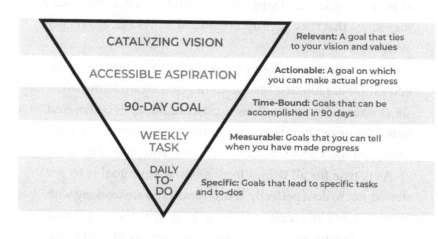

ALIGNING YOUR TIME TO MAKE PROGRESS

Once you've officially set your 90-day goals, it's time to align your actual time to those goals. This is where the rubber hits the road. It's one thing to have a lot of understanding about our Great Work, clear language to describe our goals, and a heart full of good intentions—but if we don't do something differently in the hours and minutes of our weeks and days, *we will not make progress.*

We must align the way we spend our time to our goals, tasks, and to-dos.

To share a concrete process that you can look at and imagine, I've outlined how to do in this in the *Great Work Journal,* but you can certainly do these steps in any notebook and many productivity apps.

How Can I Get a Little Closer to My Goals This Week?

At the beginning of each week, you'll review your 90-day goals and ask, "How can I get a little closer to my goals this week?" This exercise will result in three weekly tasks. Each of these tasks are concrete and substantive steps forward and are likely to take some effort over a few days. Weekly tasks often take a little research, but you're pretty sure you can figure them out.

In the first week, one of the weekly tasks Anna set for herself was to reach out to a contact she had made at a conference. He was "someone high up at the Wounded Warrior Project," and she planned to write him an email.

When she set up her weekly task in the *Great Work Journal,* she was prompted to consider, "What's likely to get in your way?" She realized that she wasn't sure what his name was, nor was she sure where to find his email. And honestly, she wasn't as up to date on the Wounded Warrior Project as she probably should be.

❯ HOW CAN I GET A LITTLE CLOSER TO MY GOALS THIS WEEK?

will move me forward?	*Reach out to my contact at Wounded Warrior*	get in my way?	*I don't know his name... or email... or anything about him*	are these blockers?	*Give myself time to dig through email, look him up and then write the email*

Under normal circumstances, people do not ask themselves this question. Instead, they state the task in its simplest form and hope for the best. For example, Anna might write, "I'll email my contact at Wounded Warrior," and then she either does nothing or buys a month-long ticket for the struggle bus.

Here's how that could look: Without acknowledging it directly, Anna feels weird that she can't remember her contact's name and hadn't kept up with his work. She questions whether it's even OK to connect with someone she hasn't kept up with.

Of course, that weirdness falls apart when looked at directly: She could just find his name and then research his organization. He wouldn't expect her to be an expert on him anyway (in fact, wouldn't it be kind of weird if she knew every detail of his work life when he'd only met her once at a conference?)! Solutions are often very simple, yet these unexamined difficulties cause can cause a lot of shame and delay.

We aren't going to let that happen.

What Is Likely to Get in My Way?

The power of asking what could go wrong and then planning around those challenges is at the heart of mental contrasting, a powerful goal-setting theory developed by Gabriele Oettingen[11]. When we set a goal and then pursue it with a dogmatic commitment to positive thinking, we are shocked and dismayed when the inevitable setbacks, mistakes, and roadblocks pop up. If, instead, we set a goal and plan for the setbacks, we get the best of both worlds.

Mental contrasting is built into every level of the *Great Work Journal*; we do it when setting goals, weekly tasks, and daily to-dos.

In Anna's case, because she didn't expect to email her contact in fifteen minutes, she was ready to do some digging.

How Can I Get a Little Closer to My Goals Today?

Even weekly tasks can be composed of mostly good intentions. The real magic happens *today. Right now.*

The daily page of the journal will prompt you: Given what you've decided to do this week, what can you do to get a little closer? I'm sure that question sounds familiar, as it's almost the same question I asked for setting weekly tasks. That's on purpose! I find that the idea of "getting a little closer" is very accessible. Most people realize that while they can't do it all today, they *can* get a little closer.

The same structure I described for setting weekly tasks governs daily to-dos. In each of the daily pages of the *Great Work Journal*, you will be asked:

- What can I do to get a little closer today?

- What will get in my way?
- How will I get around it?

Now, remember that Anna knows she's going to need to ramp up to writing her email. So, her first related to-do wasn't "Write an email to the Wounded Warrior guy." Instead, it was "Do a forensic investigation into my email and notes from that conference to figure out that guy's name and email."

What's likely to get in her way? "I have a tendency to get impatient."

How will she get around that? "I decided to keep at it for two whole hours, and if I still couldn't find it, I would start emailing other people from the conference to ask them."

☀ HOW CAN I GET A LITTLE CLOSER TO MY GOALS TODAY?

She reported back, "It only took an hour to find it! It turned out that he was copied on an email from someone else. I can do some research on Wounded Warrior tomorrow and write the email the next day! It's happening!" Look how excited she was!

Consider how differently it would have felt if every setback was a surprise. I imagine her report back would be more like "I tried to write the email, but I couldn't find his email address anywhere. Finally, *an hour later*, I found it copied in an unrelated email chain. I was like, 'Finally! Now I can write it.' And then I realized that I didn't know enough about their work, so it got delayed again. Maybe later this week, I'll finally get this email out." The email is going out on the same day in both scenarios. But the experience of it, and by association, the likelihood that the project makes further progress, is entirely different.

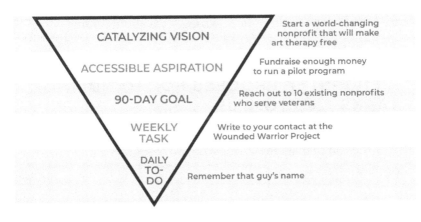

What Do I Do with All These *Other* Tasks and To-dos?

The process of using the *Great Work Method* can sound really clean and simple. You might even wonder what you'll do with yourself once these tasks and to-dos are off your list. Will you deplete your supply of ideas and be left twiddling your thumbs? Will you be so aligned that you never struggle to stay ahead of your work again? While anything is possible, I would be very surprised if this is what happened to you.

Instead, I've found that one of the fundamental problems of productivity, even when you have a rock-solid process, is how to handle this tsunami of possible tasks and to-dos that start to emerge when we get into the flow of our Great Work. No matter how committed you are to the word "no," you will still need a system to manage and prioritize potential tasks and to-dos.

I've developed a process for managing tasks that works for me. I share it with my clients and I'm sharing it with you now, in case it's helpful. Keep in mind that I share my process only as a starting point. I'm much more loose than a lot of people when it comes to my to-do list and it's OK if that doesn't work for you. It's not about right or wrong—it's about finding what works for you.

A FIVE-STEP PROCESS FOR HANDLING TASKS AND TO-DOS

I see the management of tasks and to-dos as a five-phase process:

Phase 1: Collecting. Ideas come in all the time, from every direction—from emails I receive, meetings I attend, my own brain, and in conversations—and I don't want to lose them. I describe the idea enough to jog my memory and then add them to a to-do list. I use a program that has an inbox, or a digital bin where tasks and to-dos wait to receive some more details. Most programs have a similar place where general to-dos go before you add deadlines, contexts, or people to them, but you can also just keep a simple list in a notebook or in the Notes app on your phone. Our goal in the collecting phase is just to ensure that an idea goes *somewhere* so we don't lose it.

Phase 2: Processing. When I process a task or to-do, I evaluate whether it is aligned with my goals. If it is, I'll process it further by putting it into a "project." Most to-do lists allow you to create projects so that tasks and to-dos can be separated, often even by color! I have projects for each individual goal, every client, and each class I teach.

Some people add due dates and collaborators to every task, but I usually *only* add a project. This is mostly because (as you'll see) I don't commit to doing every to-do; even the ones that are aligned with my goals may languish for weeks or months without action if they don't rise to the level of "best next step." I'm OK with that, because I want to be sure that I'm being as strategic as possible with my limited time.

If a task isn't aligned to my current goals or a project in some concrete way, I'll put it in a "parking-lot" project to be returned to at some point in the future. (Return to Chapter 3 for a reminder about long-term, medium-term, and short-term parking lots.) While the parking lots are projects according to my to-do list app, to me, they are just holding zones. I don't look at the parking lots until I'm considering new goals (or trying to remember one of my great ideas).

Phase 3: Deciding on tasks. Up until now, I've only been collecting a list of things I *could* do. I evaluate that list of potentials when I set up my week.

As we've discussed, I choose three tasks that will get me closer to my ninety-day goals. I may look at my calendar to gauge how much free time I'll have and then pick three high leverage tasks. I may pick three from the to-do list, or I may come up with three entirely different tasks.

In earlier times, I felt much more beholden to my to-do list. It was almost like I worked for my to-do list, instead of it being a tool that worked for me. Now, I try to be highly strategic, imperfect, and incomplete. And I get a lot more of what matters done, so it doesn't bother me to see things linger and eventually fade from the list. I'm not obliged to my list of to-dos! If they don't get done, but I'm making progress on what matters, I'm fine.

This is not how most people treat their to-do list, though. And if you are someone who needs to check things off the list so you can sleep at night, then you might want to process your tasks with more fervor. Delete things off the list as soon as possible. Be vigilant with that "No!" And give yourself the gift of at least one parking-lot project, where you decide in advance that these tasks and to-dos aren't even *allowed* to get done!

Phase 4: Delegating. If a task is fairly straightforward and aligned to my goals, I'll ask: Should I do this, or is there someone else who could do it for me? If possible, I delegate the meat of it and then replace the original task with the task of managing the delegation. (I.e., "Order T-shirts for the boot camp" becomes "Ask my assistant to order T-shirts for the boot camp.")

Keep in mind that once you delegate a task, your task of managing your assistant's work is now non-negotiable. If you aren't ready to commit to the larger project, you might want to wait before delegating the task, or you could find yourself (as I have!) with a task done by an assistant for a project that has been put on hold.

Phase 5: Doing. Once a task makes it into the weekly page of the *Great Work Journal*, I will look at my calendar and see when I can make progress. My calendar is already populated with appointments; client meetings, doctor appointments, classes I teach, and my standing writing time are all already blocked on my calendar. On any given day, I will look at my time and choose three to-dos.

Unless my day is packed, I don't designate appointments as one of my three to-dos for that day. If my day *is* packed with appointments, I will almost always make one of my to-dos this one: "Be present with my appointments and take any unexpected time off as a break." Because I don't like super-packed days, this happens less and less often.

This system allows me to collect and then control the tsunami of incoming tasks while still moving my goals forward. Here's an example:

I'm walking down the street when it occurs to me, *I should write an article for Quartz entailed Leading for Greatness about how to encourage Great Work in teams!* I take out my phone and drop it into the bin on my time management program.

Later that week I'm processing the bin on OmniFocus, and see my article idea. I realize that while the idea is truly a good one, I'm not writing articles right now. I will be next quarter, though, so for now the idea goes into medium term parking.

As I'm setting up my goals the next quarter, I decide that writing three articles would be a great way to promote my new course. I pull ideas out of the parking lots and assign them to my "Write Three Articles" project, including this one about *Leading for Greatness*. I delete a few ideas as I'm moving them, because though they sounded good at first, they've aged like a bad cheese. I'm so glad that I didn't try to move on them right away!

A few weeks later, I've decided to outline an article to work it up to pitch. As I'm going through ideas in the project, I'm struck by how good this *Leading for Greatness* idea is and think it could be the winner. I add *"Write an outline for article on Leading for Greatness"* into the weekly page of my Great Work Journal.

Throughout the week, I set a few individual to-dos, like "Read a few articles on vision for teams" and "Choose three points to highlight in the article." Before long, the outline is written and off to the editorial team at Quartz, where it will surely win an award for cutting edge journalism.

MAKING SURE YOUR DAILY TO-DOS ARE ALIGNED WITH YOUR BIGGER ASPIRATIONS AND VISION

WHAT HAPPENS WHEN WE HAVE a great idea that feels doable, but we aren't sure whether it *matters*? Leaving Anna out of this for a minute, let's say that it occurs to you to ask Matt for help with your budget. Matt's a nice guy, and he's likely very willing to help, but is this something that is worth his and your time? How would we know?

Well, when your time is aligned, the daily to-do will link all the way to a vision. For example:

- The to-do—asking for Matt's help—may very well be tied into a weekly **task** of creating a budget draft.
- The budget draft weekly task is tied to a **90-day goal** of figuring how to work from a budget.

- This makes sense, because you are hell-bent on making a profit in your business this year (**accessible aspiration**).
- Why? Because secretly, *someday* you want a seven-figure (that's a MILLION-dollar) company. (**Vision!**)

This idea is aligned to your goal, and is approved for addition to a daily page of the *Great Work Journal!*

A RETURN TO THE LAND OF "NO"

Now, LET'S SAY YOU GET the idea to build a pergola in your backyard. You fall down a Google rabbit hole and discover that it really wouldn't be that hard! You can get everything you need delivered from Home Depot by four p.m. You start imagining yourself in your backyard having a cookout in the shade of your new pergola. People will be amazed that you made it with your own hands! And you love it when people are amazed.

Then, just before you hit that orange "buy" button, you stop and ask, "Is this a high-leverage project? Is it aligned with my long-term hopes and dreams?"

As you try to tie it to a stretch, support, or sanity goal, or even to an aspiration or vision, you come up empty. It's a good idea! It would be a nice accomplishment! And people might just be amazed, but it's not a great idea that will get you closer to what you really want. And so, like some marketer's nightmare, you abandon your $800 Home Depot cart and get back to the things you said you would do.

Just to be clear, I'm not against pergolas! If you are in the middle of flipping your house because you want to sell it at a massive profit and move to Taos, New Mexico, and start your alternative health store, *Crystal Empire*, then I say, "Go for it!" But it's much too easy to find all our limited time consumed by one-off, random projects that feel good for a minute and then become obligations. Or, maybe more likely, half-finished disappointments.

This process of assessing whether your daily to-dos are aligned with your longer-term goals, aspirations, and vision is very helpful to keep you grounded in your Great Work. It helps keep you from being jerked around by small tasks that may or may not actually accumulate into what you are truly hoping to accomplish.

In this way, your 90-day goals will operate like constraints. For the next ninety days at least, you will say "no" to the ideas that are good, but not Great. You will align your time today to your 90-day goals, so your effort can accumulate, and you can finally do what matters most.

GREAT WORK GENERATES GREAT WORK

ANNA'S EMAIL TO HER CONNECTION at Wounded Warrior earned her a virtual coffee. During their conversation, her contact suggested she reach out to someone he knew at Operation Second Chance. Her new friend at Operation Second Chance introduced her to someone she didn't know in another division at the VA. About six months later, her new colleague at the VA offered Anna a promotion to move into an integrative health clinic that included art therapy among its offerings.

Anna was intrigued, surprised, and not at all sure what to do. If she took the new role, her dream of starting her own nonprofit would be delayed at best and derailed at worst. But the new role involved learning fundraising, and her new co-workers were passionate and interesting practitioners who saw the benefits of alternative treatments, just as she did.

What to do?

These are good problems to have! And they are, without a doubt, the kind of problems you encounter when you get into the flow of your Great Work. It is messy, exciting, and non-linear, involving unexpected opportunities and chances to change direction. In fact, part of the fun is the unpredictable and emerging nature of it. That didn't make Anna's decision any easier, but it was gratifying to know that whichever choice she made, she would still be doing her Great Work.

Anna opted to take the role in the integrative health clinic. And, at the time of this writing, she's glad she did. "I've learned a lot about fundraising, and I've had my eyes opened to a lot of other therapies, like acupuncture and hypnosis, that are also really powerful for veterans. When I do start my nonprofit, which I'm still planning to do, I think it will be even better."

In the next chapter, we will dive into the flow of your Great Work. It turns out that crafting your own recipe of successful strategies—formulated from what I like to call "self-expertise"—makes the twists and turns of Great Work much easier to navigate with ease and confidence.

CHAPTER FIVE

DISCOVER HOW YOU, *SPECIFICALLY*, DO GREAT WORK

"To thine own self be true."

*William Shakespeare, celebrating more than 400 years
as the "greatest writer in the English language"*

SINCE ENDING HIS MILITARY CAREER, Peter has been crushing it as a freelance video copywriter. He writes scripts and edits videos for entrepreneurs and small companies. His work includes introductory videos for websites, social media reels, sales sequences videos, and video lead magnets. He's got a knack for taking on the voice of the company that hired him and scripting compelling stories, clear examples, and powerful outcomes. He can charge a lot of money for this skillset, and it's been a long time since he's worried about finding work. In fact, he's gotten so good at it, he's actually a little bored. He's ready to do something of his own.

"I've had this interesting screenplay idea for the past year or two, but I've been so busy working on other people's projects that I haven't had the bandwidth to develop it. I worked like crazy for the past six or eight months to get a little cushion, and now I'm taking a hiatus for a few months so I can just focus on the screenplay. The problem is, when I sit down to work on it, I freeze.

"I worked so hard to buy myself this time and now I can't make any headway. I'm very concerned that this time is going to slip away from me, and I'll be back where I began."

Peter is facing a common dilemma. Basically, "What got you here, won't get you there." When the nature of the work you're doing changes, or the context of the work shifts, the way you do that work will also change. Most of us get locked into a single way of working and living. We think that there is a right way, and once we've found it, we hold on tight. This can lead to frustration and a lot of lost time. To shake it off, we have to loosen our hold on "the how" and get experimental.

Though it can feel uncomfortable at first, being experimental is a skill we've all had. Every one of us began our lives as meandering children, living in the moment and responding to the world around us as it evolved. We were natural experimenters with an unbridled curiosity about the way the world worked.

And then we went to school.

That's when our natural meandering curiosity was replaced by a rigid schedule where we were expected to show interest in math at ten twenty-five every day for exactly thirty-five minutes. At that point, our curiosity should turn on a dime and be directed toward stories, or spelling, or gym.

These rigid expectations at school extended far beyond scheduling. We wrote essays that were graded to a rubric, thereby shaping and narrowing our understanding of quality. We learned facts in such a way as to answer multiple-choice questions, a form of testing that greatly limits our ability to critically examine nuance. We accepted the need for silence when we wanted to talk and stillness when we wanted to move, and we learned to force our attention when we were bored. (Or we don't, and then we get left behind or drop out—but that's a rant for a different book.) In short, most of us fell in line. In doing so, we were directed to look outside ourselves to find the right, approved, and sanctioned way to behave.

The point here is not to argue that schools are wrong, or that kids shouldn't sit still, or that tests have hijacked our schools, but just to notice that we learn from a very early age that our natural way of being—our inclinations and our preferences—aren't that important when it comes to what the world expects of us.

For Peter, this was compounded in the military. A more hierarchical, top-down, and structured organization would be hard to find. This comes with a lot of benefits! People know what to do, when to do it, and how to communicate with an efficiency that *saves lives.* They also stop listening to the part of themselves that would prefer to sleep later, argue small points, or have more agency over their projects at work. It is, perhaps, a necessity. And, like all good and necessary things, it comes with consequences.

Following our instincts, developing our own schedule, accepting our preferences, and leveraging our strengths are no longer our natural inclination, is my point. This is especially true if you are a rule-follower, a people-pleaser, an A+ student, or a good soldier. These tendencies make you very coachable (a good thing!) *and* unduly afraid to "waste time" on trying things that "might not work." If you are dedicated to excellence, a fan of best practices and step-by-step instructions, and a great admirer of high performers, then you are in the right place. It's time to recover the lost art of giving things a try.

GREAT WORK REQUIRES SELF-EXPERTISE

WHEN YOU ARE READY TO dig deep and do your Great Work, this reliance on finding and dogmatically adhering to a right way becomes a liability. This is a cruel twist of fate, because for decades it was a great asset. Maybe one of your greatest!

Nonetheless, Great Work requires that you learn how to find your own way. This doesn't mean you need to throw the baby out with the bathwater and start from scratch, eschewing everything you've learned from others. We definitely do not have time for that.

Instead, we are seeking a middle ground, where we learn what we can from others, and then adjust what we learn to our own unique perspective and needs. There is much to be learned from common sense, standard advice, and others' suggestions. Learn as much as you can, by all means! And then, inevitably, there will come a time when you realize that all advice needs to be seen as just that: advice. Experiments to try.

Should you get up at five a.m. and do "deep work" before anything else? Maybe.

Should you "eat the frog," and do the hard stuff before the mundane stuff? Maybe.

Should you use time blocking? The Pomodoro method? Inbox Zero? Freedom.to? A to-do list? A calendaring link for remote scheduling?

All of these ideas receive a resounding: "Maybe!"

Regarding these ideas and all the others that come your way, my recommendation is to try them out and see. In doing these experiments, you'll develop what will become the true driver of your own Great Work: self-expertise.

WHAT IS SELF-EXPERTISE?

SELF-EXPERTISE IS THE COLLECTION OF knowledge about what it takes for *you* to make change in *your own life.*

- When do you do your best work?
- How do you prefer to collaborate?
- How do you recover from overwork?
- What invigorates you and makes you feel alive?
- What time of day is your energy so low that you double the time it takes to make progress?
- Who do you love to bounce ideas off of?

The answers to these questions (and others) comprise your secret recipe for Great Work; or, what I call self-expertise. Some of these strategies will align with "best practices" and some of them will contradict them. Some of them will be unusual and surprising, while others will be very mundane and ordinary. The thing that ties these strategies together is *you:* your particular way of being, and your specific needs, history, and perspective.

The secret recipe of self-expertise is personal and intimate, and it doesn't need to make sense to anyone else. There are a *lot* of suggestions out there about what works for productivity and what doesn't. And, not surprisingly, some of those tips contradict one another. Should you do Deep Work before all else? Or should you ease into your day? No one person could do both, of course.

It's not a surprise that there are two conflicting pieces of "common knowledge," because neither idea is right or wrong—instead, each is a good fit for some people and not for others. Almost everything, even strategies that feel like they are based on cold, hard facts, won't work for everyone.

For example, one of the things that we know *for sure* about the human brain is that it hates to switch between tasks[12]. Since we lose a little bit of our willpower and focus every time we switch tasks, we know that if we multi-task for long, we will end up confused, depleted, and wondering why we procrastinate so much.

This. Is. True.

And yet, my good friend Gil loves, loves, loves to multi-task! I was so adamant and so persuasive that multi-tasking doesn't work that he agreed to do an experiment where he didn't multi-task for a whole week. During that week, he made a strong effort to time block and single-track, instead.

Here's what he told me at the end of the week:

"I feel a little dead inside. It was like walking through molasses all week! I never got up to a gallop. I understand that the 'Deep Work[13]' I did was maybe better... but I was soooo bored. Sorry, Amanda. I'm going back to multi-tasking."

And you know what? As much as it pains me to say this, Gil *should* ignore my advice. He should absolutely go ahead and multi-task because that's what works for him!

What works for you can only be discovered by trying things out. Even my suggestions—though grounded in research and offered with a pure heart—are just that: suggestions. Let this book and every other blog, article, and podcast on productivity you encounter be a source of ideas for developing your secret recipe of self-expertise—not a mandate on what works for high performance.

To uncover your own self-expertise, I suggest a three-part cycle:

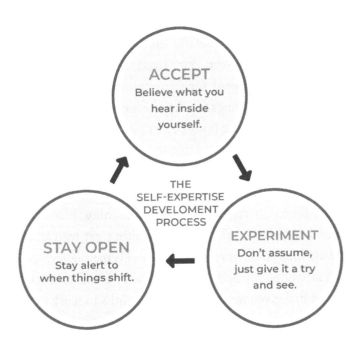

Step 1: Accept What's True About You

Peter and I met at a conference several years ago when we were both attending a session on habits. Because of his history in the military, Peter found habit research very compelling.

"It was like getting the user manual for civilian productivity. It was practical and straightforward and didn't require much talent—just willpower for the first few weeks." Routines, structures, and adherence to clearly articulated standards are hallmarks of the military's training style, and Peter was comfortable with it.

One particular habit that resonated with Peter was time blocking—creating blocks on your calendar for particular tasks. Often, it is recommended that you block creative time or "deep work" first thing in the morning, and then have meetings and phone calls blocked in the early afternoon when your energy and focus might be lower. Peter lived by time blocking—he would exercise, then work for about four hours, and then take phone calls and meetings for the afternoon. He would check email once a day, in the hour before he signed off. It worked like clockwork *for years*.

Until it didn't.

"When I decided to write my screenplay, things went haywire. I'd sit down to write in the morning, like I always do, and I couldn't concentrate. I couldn't get into it. I was procrastinating, and I never procrastinate! It was like some other person inhabited my body for those hours. It was excruciating because I had given myself only four months to work without other writing projects. That was a big financial risk! And then, suddenly, I couldn't work. It was terrifying."

For almost a month, Peter tried to fit into his old pattern. Eventually, however, he had to accept that diving right into his screenplay at seven a.m. wasn't working. Once he did, he opened the door to experiments that would reveal what *would* work.

THE IMPORTANCE OF BELIEVING WHAT YOU HEAR

One of the most important skills involved in doing
Great Work is finding the voice inside you that speaks the
inconvenient, unconventional, and (at times) terrifying truth.

Find that voice of truth, and clear the static from its signal.

Listen to it, and practice believing what you hear.

"This isn't working. Try this instead."

If you listen and establish enough trust with yourself,
you'll learn to hear your clear "no" even when you think you
should say "yes," and your clear "yes" even when you are
scared. That one skill alone can make pursuing your
Great Work much easier.

Step 2: Don't Assume. Experiment

Once Peter accepted that his status quo wasn't working for
him, he needed to discover what did. I encouraged him to just
try things out, and boy, did he!

- He tried writing at five a.m. *before* he went to the gym.
  ("I never got to the gym!")
- He tried reading something related to his project before
  writing. ("I got pulled into the articles and ended up

making lots of notes, which was helpful… but it was hard to get to the actual writing part.")
- He tried writing in public, at a coffee shop. ("It was so distracting! I kept getting pulled into other people's conversations.")
- He tried calling his mother before beginning to write. ("Talk about stressful.")
- He tried listening to music. Without music. With the TV on. With noise-canceling headphones.

Eventually, he hit on a solution that worked. When he returns from the gym, he sits down (before his shower—TMI, I know, and I'm sorry, but details matter!) and sets a timer for fifteen minutes. Then, blasphemy! He checks his email.

"It sort of turns my brain on for a minute, but in a fifteen-minute increment, it doesn't drag me in," Peter explained. "Then, after my shower, I blare some music and read what I wrote the day before while I take notes on a legal pad with a pen. I do this in my bedroom, which seems to matter.

"Then, I grab my coffee and head to my home office, sit down, turn off all the other computer programs (especially email!), turn on distraction-free writing, continue the blaring music… and I can write! It's not the same as the writing I did before. It doesn't pour out of me in the same way, but I'm making progress, and it feels great!"

Step 3: Don't Be Rigid: Stay Open and Allow for Movement over Time

The most effective productivity habits are the ones that work for you right now. Peter was surrounded by people who swore by writing before checking email, before taking a meeting, before *anything* except working out or doing morning pages. It worked for him, too, for almost a decade. But when it came time to do his own Great Work, it didn't jive anymore. He tried and tried to fit into the old pattern, and that rigidity lost him almost a whole month of his precious hiatus.

It's better to try new things as soon as it feels like the system is breaking down. Don't force yourself to be who you were before and do what you did before, and most of all, let go of what other people think you should be doing! Instead, access that voice inside you and believe what you are hearing as quickly as possible. Then, Let. It. Go.

When you are flexible and open to adjustment, something *will* eventually work. And what a relief it will be! When something works after nothing was working, it feels great! Run with it!

Of course, you want to be careful not to assume that you've finally figured it out forever and always. Nothing works forever, including the thing that is working like gangbusters right now. Maintain your self-reflective practice and stay open to shifting in both small and large ways.

Because things will change. *You* will change. Sometimes dramatically! Think about the parents who were night owls before becoming morning people when their baby was born. Think about people who start working an overnight shift and are suddenly most creative when they used to be braindead. And sometimes, like Peter discovered, a shift from doing work we are assigned to doing our own Great Work, can prompt us to shift our habits in more nuanced ways.

When these things happen, it's time to begin the cycle again.

EXAMPLES OF WHERE SELF-EXPERTISE IS ESPECIALLY HELPFUL

LET'S LOOK AT A COUPLE examples of common areas where self-expertise and experimentation are especially helpful: developing a gratitude practice, discovering the timing of our Hours of Greatness, and learning how to maintain wellness while doing Great Work.

Self-Expertise Required: Hours of Greatness

Remember our discussion about motivation in Chapter 2? How some work is intrinsically motivated, emerging from interest, curiosity, and long-term hopes and dreams? And how some work is extrinsically motivated, emerging from things like expectations, duty, and fear? We then focused on the competitive advantage you get from bringing more intrinsic motivation into your work.

In this chapter, we need to talk about the different energetic footprints of these differently motivated tasks. Extrinsically motivated work (from outside of you) is easier. It takes less energy, and because we are more objective about what's needed, we don't question our own ability to do it as often. Extrinsically motivated work causes *much less drama*, because it matters so much less to us.

Compare that to work for which the motivation comes largely from inside ourselves (intrinsically motivated work). Intrinsically motivated work is the foundation of Great Work, and it takes a lot out of you. We care about doing it well, which can lead to perfectionism, and we worry that we don't have what it takes, which can lead to procrastination. It takes effort and willpower to overcome these two urges. One of the most powerful ways to find the energy to do your Great Work, despite its toll, is to optimize your schedule as much as possible to your energetic tendencies. One such tendency is when your Hours of Greatness occur.

Hours of Greatness are those mythical hours during the day when we are best able to do the deep, thoughtful work required to create something Great. This kind of work takes a lot more energy *and* a greater degree of willpower, so you want to do them when your energy is at its highest.

To discover your Hours of Greatness, ask yourself this question: When do I have the most energy during the day?

There are two relatively standard patterns (though you may not fit into either of them, and that's OK—remember, listen to yourself, and believe what you hear):

Hours of Greatness Profile: The Early Bird

This is the most widespread pattern; I fit it, and so does Peter. When you are an early bird, your best creative time is first thing in the morning. You may or may not need some ramping-up time after you wake up, but once you get going, the first four-ish hours of your day are the most creative, the most productive, and the most energized. Peter and I sometimes talk about how we wish we could justify getting up at three a.m. to extend this time for maximum effect. But alas, our spouses and my kids frown upon us going to bed at seven p.m.

Hours of Greatness Profile: The Night Owl

Chloe, who we met in Chapter 3, has the opposite pattern. She wakes up at the last possible moment, goes to work in a haze, and slowly ramps up until about eleven a.m. Then she comes to life, taking great meetings and working with others until she comes home. Then, at around nine or ten p.m., she lights up. Her creativity comes online, and, as she says, "I'm suddenly hitting on all cylinders. I work like that until about one a.m., but if I didn't have a regular job, I bet I would work from eleven until two or three in the morning and then sleep until ten or eleven." For her, ten p.m. is when her Great Work comes most quickly, her energy bubbles away, and her best ideas flow.

This is so foreign to me. By ten p.m., I'm so braindead I can't even watch TV! And whether I can understand Chloe's Night Owl profile matters *not at all*. What matters is that it works for her.

SELF-EXPERTISE SHOULD GUIDE YOUR SCHEDULE WHENEVER POSSIBLE

People are different, is my point, and that's OK. No, it's better than OK—it's great! The key is to *accept it,* and then experiment to create a schedule that makes you feel in tune for most of your day. When you are working in this way, your progress will accelerate, and it will feel good instead of stressful to stretch into your Great Work.

When you don't work in this aligned way, you may feel out of sorts a lot of the time. For example, if you spend your creative time answering emails and doing internet research, you are not only wasting your Hours of Greatness—which is a shame—but you will likely feel weirdly deflated. You had all this potential energy, but you gave it nowhere to go. In my experience, that feels gross.

Similarly, trying to force yourself to do challenging, intense work when your energy is low is also uncomfortable and painfully inefficient, because it requires *a lot* of extra willpower. For me, I completely flag between two p.m. and four p.m. The lowest point for my energy is three p.m. If I need to write, or plan, or convince anyone of anything, three p.m. is not the right time.

These days, as I've gotten my schedule almost entirely under my sole control, I usually meditate at two-thirty and then hang out with the kids at three. Of course, there are times when I need to force myself to take a meeting or work on a creative project during the afternoon flag... and I *can* do that! It just takes longer, feels like forcing, and leaves me depleted.

Working against your natural schedule is OK once in a while, but it's no way to live.

And yet *so many people* live like this!

Scheduling in a manner that recognizes and capitalizes on your Hours of Greatness profile is one of the most powerful adjustments you can make to your life. If you are able to work whenever you want, wherever you want, and in whatever order works for you, you have keys to great productivity at your fingertips.

Oddly, despite this freedom, even most entrepreneurs I know are keeping themselves on a very traditional schedule built around other people's convenience. They schedule meetings all day, and try to fit in their Great Work into the pockets that happen to occur on their calendar. Usually, they get up early *and* do work late at night. And while almost any energetic pattern can be normal, I don't meet very many people (OK, I've never met a single person) who are equally effective at five a.m. as eleven p.m.

Even if, like most people, you have a job where your company sets your hours, you can exert more control than you realize. With effort, you can usually shape your calendar a lot more than you think. You can block fake conference calls to create a sacred block of time during at least part of your Hours of Greatness. You can suggest meetings at particular times of day. You can ask to start or end your day a little earlier or a little later. You can ask for exceptions, and you just might get them!

In all my time as a coach, and despite *all the pushback* I've gotten from people in competitive, corporate, and billable industries, I've never met anyone who couldn't *do something* about their schedule. I know you can, too.

SUCCESSFUL COLLABORATION: WHEN EVERYONE'S SELF-EXPERTISE MATTERS

WHILE IT IS VERY, EXTREMELY, critically important that you develop your own self-expertise, it is also important that you resist becoming dogmatic and rigid about it when you are collaborating with others. The benefits of self-expertise don't require that your preferences always rule the day. Instead, knowing your particularities allows you to compromise more strategically, ensuring that the workflow is viable for all parties. The benefits of collaboration are massive, and figuring out how to work well with others is beyond the scope of this book. For now, I just want to be sure we are being judicious in the way we are using our self-expertise.

Here's an example of what *not* to do:

You learn that your Hours of Greatness occur between eight and eleven a.m. You protect them with your life and refuse to do anything else during that time. Normally, this is fine, because almost all of life is more flexible than we think. But then, your best friend, or your mother, or your husband asks you to go with him or her to the doctor to discuss a possible cancer diagnosis at nine a.m. You refuse, asserting that you "can't" because you "must honor your Hours of Greatness."

Here's another example of what not to do:

A colleague has asked you to collaborate on the most exciting project at your company. He has an opposite energetic profile from you, so he is always asking you to have a meeting at ten a.m. when his energy is low. You want to have meetings in the afternoon, but that's when he's heads down doing his own Great Work. What to do?

Do not insist that all of the meetings are on your schedule and turn this into a full-scale "thing" where you feel disrespected because he continues asking you for meetings at four p.m. Having self-expertise is not an excuse to blow things out of proportion.

At the same time, you don't have to acquiesce completely to his preferences and make all the meetings at his convenience. Instead, talk to your colleague! Surface your preferences and discuss them openly. You can say, "I prefer to have meetings in the afternoon, and you seem to prefer to have them in the morning. What should we do? Do you think lunchtime is the sweet spot? Or do you think it's better to alternate?"

Transparent communication is one of the best parts of self-expertise; when you know what you want, you are better able to negotiate with others effectively to reach a solution that meets your needs, *and theirs*.

Self-expertise is not meant to be a tool for rigidity, pathologizing (thinking everything is a disease and therefore outside of your control), or manipulation. It is, instead, an instrument of efficiency and compassion.

The most compassionate collaborations start when everyone shares their self-expertise. This allows us to find a path forward that will mostly work for everyone, most of the time. When no one's individual preferences rule the day, we become open to the magic that happens when people join forces.

SELF-EXPERTISE FOR WELLNESS: FORTIFICATION AND INVIGORATION

PETER MADE GREAT STRIDES BY optimizing his day to the emerging needs of his new screenplay project.

But that's not the whole story.

To take his hiatus, Peter had to generate extra time and money. To do this, he took on about 20 percent more work than usual through the earlier months of the year, and then worked feverishly to wrap every client project ahead of schedule. "I worked every night and weekend all year to carve out this time. That's why I was so nervous when I wasn't getting any traction."

In addition to the need to shift his habits, there is also a much more mundane explanation for Peter's struggle: He was tired. In the run up to his hiatus, Peter allowed all his self-care and wellness practices to slide. He wasn't exercising. He wasn't eating very well. And he wasn't meditating, watching funny TV shows, going out with friends, or even reading for fun. By the time he got to his hiatus he was exhausted—physically, emotionally, and mentally.

He needed a break.

I see wellness as encompassing two broad categories of self-care. The first, which I call "fortification," involves ensuring our baseline health and resilience. This usually involves moving and resting our bodies, eating good food, getting enough sleep and downtime, and spending at least some time in the company of other people we enjoy. Out of this category of self-care comes mental, emotional, and cognitive health.

The second broad category of wellness, is what I call "invigoration." When we experience at least a baseline threshold of health, we begin to yearn for things that excite us. This can involve adventures to new places, opportunities to eat new food and try new activities, or projects that challenge us to dig deeper and contribute more. Of course, it also involves pursuing our Great Work.

Peter arrived at his hiatus badly in need of fortification. But, instead of giving himself a short rest so that he could be in top form for the invigoration of his Great Work project, he just dove right in.

"I don't have time to rest," he told me. And I could understand where he was coming from. How could I argue that he spend even one day of his hiatus not working on his screenplay?

And yet, as he pushed forward, the ideas didn't flow. The project felt stuck, and he felt stymied. Some of this, as we've already discussed, is because he needed a new workflow, but some of it is because he had depleted all his resilience.

Resilience, as you may remember from our discussion of sanity goals, is your well of strength from which Great Work flows. Resilience depends greatly on you being foundationally fortified—rested, fed, and emotionally stable. Without resilience, everything is hard, all you want to be is done, and every obstacle feels insurmountable. When your resilience is strong, on the other hand, the same things feel manageable, you will naturally think more deeply and more creatively about your work, and new ideas and solutions to problems will come to you out of nowhere.

When we are depleted, we can struggle along and eke out progress, like Peter, one painful word at a time. Or we can stop, take a real break, recover more deeply (and more quickly) and then return to our work with a renewed sense of excitement and access to our best thinking.

I've found that accomplishing things when I'm exhausted is so difficult that it actually takes longer than stopping, taking a real break, recovering my enthusiasm, and *then* returning to the task.

"It's no accident that the best idea I've ever had in my life—perhaps maybe the best one I'll ever have in my life—came to me on vacation." He continued, "The moment my brain got a moment's rest, *Hamilton* walked into it."

Lin Manuel Miranda,
creator of the wildly popular musical, **Hamilton**

As Peter struggled to get his writing groove back, he instinctively returned to prior self-care practices. He had some downtime while he was procrastinating. He started going to the gym again during his experiments. He adjusted his eating away from convenience foods and got back into cooking. In addition to figuring out a new set of habits, Peter rested and recovered. And then, like clockwork, he felt the call to invigoration.

Protecting our baseline health and wellness is something that absolutely needs to come from self-expertise. This is one area where all the "tried and true" methods must be tried and found true *by you*. Rigorous exercise, for example, is deeply relaxing to some people, and to others, it is a great source of stress. The exact foods that nourish us and make us feel good in our bodies is deeply personal. Whether to set rigid boundaries between home and work or allow it to be more fluid depends entirely on which one makes you feel more resilient. All these insights, and more, come from developing self-expertise.

Suffice to say, I don't presume to tell you *how* to care for your baseline health. I do presume to tell you, however, that if you want to do Great Work, then you must take care of your health to ensure your resilience. I suppose you can grind your way through work that doesn't matter (*not recommended*), but doing Great Work depends on you having full access to your creativity, problem-solving abilities, and can-do attitude. All of these rely on resilience.

It's not always the case that the missing self-care component is part of foundational health. Nadine, a program coordinator in a government job, was taking *very good* care of herself. She was exercising, eating well, meditating, and spending time with her friends every weekend. As I stood in awe of her immaculate makeup and her Michelle Obama arms, she let me in on the secret: "I have all the time in the world, because my job is *so boring*. But I can't get a new one because I'm only two years away from having my student loans paid off for my public service! I do feel like I'm just wasting my life away in this cubicle," she said.

Nadine needed some invigoration. She needed a way to feel excited and engaged about something substantive in her life again. Since there was nothing at work to excite her, she needed to look outside of work. When probed, she told me that she had always been interested in cosplay and had, during her college years, made costumes for her friends to use. For the uninformed, like me, cosplay is where groups of people get together in very extravagant costumes. I'm not talking about a hat and mask. I'm talking about full replicas of Queen Elizabeth's gowns, or skintight leather superhero outfits. Or, my favorite, the retro-futuristic steampunk jackets that look like a cross between early industrial era clothes and fast fashion. Apparently, Nadine could make all these things.

I encouraged her to do so again. Not because it was going to get her somewhere but because she would find it fun. She would make interesting friends and be valued again for her creativity and panache. That's enough, all by itself, to make us feel better and less bored. I've heard that she has made quite a name for herself in New York's cosplay community, *and* she had her loans paid off by working at her boring job. So, I sent her an email asking for an update.

Nadine said, "Oddly, doing the cosplay stuff made me much less bored at work. I mean the job was still boring, but I didn't care as much because I had something else on my mind."

I hear this all the time. Doing even a little bit of Great Work, whether it's within your career or outside of your career altogether, can make life feel exciting again. Emerging from the morass of boredom that was consuming us, we find friends, projects, and interesting things to talk about. Often people think that if they aren't going to do something "seriously" (usually code for "as a career"), they think it isn't worth doing at all.

I couldn't disagree more. Great Work as a self-care practice can be just as satisfying as doing Great Work in your career. But, like everything else, it requires self-expertise. It will take experimentation to figure out what will make you feel excited, and how to ensure that you don't end up overcommitted and stressed out.

GRATITUDE: HOW ANTICIPATION, SAVORING, AND REMINISCING MAKE YOU HAPPIER

SELF-EXPERTISE ABOUT WELLNESS IS NOT only about solving problems when things aren't working. In fact, some of the most powerful self-expertise is about what works! One positive habit that you'll want to figure out how to harness is the practice of gratitude.

According to Fred Bryant and Joseph Veroff in their book *Savoring*[14], there are three kinds of gratitude: gratitude for things that you hope and expect to happen, called *anticipation*; gratitude for something that is happening right now, called *savoring*; and gratitude for what has already happened, called *reminiscence*.

Each of these three practices will operate differently for each of us, depending on our natural tendencies. You will discover that some things raise your emotion and generate gratitude quickly, while other things fall flat and feel empty.

For some people, focusing on big moments of joy in their own life, such as reminiscing about their wedding day, is a sure-fire way to generate feelings of gratitude. For others, the real gratitude comes from thinking about smaller, ordinary moments, like when your partner brings you a cup of coffee or you get a great parking spot. For still others, gratitude for things that happen to others you love, such as when your sister called you to tell that she got a new job, generate waves of gratitude. As you practice anticipation, savoring, and reminiscence across the many moments of your life, you will learn what works best to bring on the gratitude.

Across the board, the goal of a gratitude practice is to bring your attention to the positive details of your experience in a way that taps into emotion and evokes feelings of satisfaction, happiness, or joy. When anticipating, imagine the pride swelling in your chest as you hold your yet unwritten book in your hands for the first time. When savoring, notice the curl of your daughter's hair, or the look on your manager's face when you tell her you got the deal. When you are reminiscing, remember the warm feel of the cup of coffee in your cold hands. Whenever you are engaging in gratitude, focus on these smaller details, as they evoke a deeper emotional connection than simply thinking about the overall memory.

Try it for yourself! Bring to mind something for which you are grateful. It can be a family member you love, an accomplishment you are proud of, or a lovely experience you had. Let your self-expertise guide you.

Let's say that you are grateful for the fact that you live close to the ocean. Starting right there, think "I'm grateful that I live so close to the ocean." And you might just feel a little surge of satisfaction in your chest.

Now, let's add details "I'm glad I live close enough to drive past the ocean three times a day. I love to stop, get out of the car, stand on the sand, and admire the vastness of the ocean. Or I can close my eyes and listen, hearing seagulls overhead and the crash of the waves down below." Visualizing this experience, in all its specificity, allows you to feel the deep peace you get when you are near the ocean. Can you feel the difference?

The push to generate details, as well as the recommendation that you re-activate your gratitude multiple times, is because *this is how* gratitude hacks your brain. You see, your brain (and mine) has a strong negativity bias[15]. Researchers estimate that your brain will return to a negative experience between four and ten times more often than it will return to a positive experience. Some of this negativity bias comes from our protective instincts to stay safe, but some of it comes from simple habit. Memories that we revisit are strengthened. That strengthening means that they are more likely to be visited again, even without your conscious intent.

A gratitude practice activates our positive memories several times. Anticipating a positive experience gives our positive memory a strong, connected starting place. Paying attention to the details as good things occur in the moment creates a strong memory trace to return to. Re-activating the memory and the connected emotions while reminiscing allows us to "prime" these positive memories so they occur to us again even without our conscious effort.

My son recently decided that he wanted to learn to play the guitar. As such, we bought him an electric guitar (or a "rock guitar" as he calls it) and signed him up for lessons at the School of Rock. Their program, just like in the movie, is designed around a live performance. Every week, he goes for one private lesson and one group performance lesson. The performance is based around a particular artist or style of music. Alex chose a performance program focused on the Beatles. Suddenly, my home was ringing with the harmonies of "Let it Be," "Yellow Submarine," "Come Together," and "Hey Jude." About halfway through the program, Alex asked if he could sing in the performance, to which they agreed. Alex and I both thought that this was *very good news*, and I made it my business to savor all of it while it was happening.

I brought my attention to the details:

- I appreciated the excitement in Alex's voice when he said, "Hey Siri, play 'Come Together.'"
- As a family, we spent an entire afternoon listening to the Beatles' top hits. We discovered that while most of us appreciate Paul McCartney's songwriting, Alex naturally leaned toward John Lennon. I noticed that Alex took pride in being the only one who could fully appreciate the grittier and more personal lyrics of John Lennon.
- I put my arm around Alex as he and I sat on his bed practicing his songs. The feeling of his little body, shaking as he projected his voice to sing loud and proud, brought tears to my eyes.

If savoring is about being fully aware of the goodness as it occurs, anticipation is about looking forward to a lovely moment before it occurs. In the weeks leading up to the performance, I shared stories with Alex of my own performance experiences. We bought Beatles shirts for all of us to wear to the performance. I rallied our friends and family, providing a link and a few reminders so they could watch his performance over Zoom. I told everyone at work how excited I was to attend his performance. And, on the day of his performance, we practiced, got dressed in Beatles shirts, and cheered when we dropped him off at rehearsal.

After his performance, we intentionally reminisced as a family over dinner. We reviewed the performance, sharing our favorite moments. We sang the songs again, and asked Alex what it was like for him, allowing him to reminisce, too. Since then, whenever one of us wears our Beatles shirt, we tell a story from his performance, reigniting those memories and experiencing gratitude all over again.

All of these intentional efforts help us to see all that our lives have to offer, and will fundamentally change our perception of our lives, seeing it more positively. So, when we activate *and re-activate* positive memories, we will perceive our life as more positive *and we will be happier,* even if nothing else changes.

Of course, it's not like nothing else will change. In fact, other things *definitely will* change. Gratitude makes us happier, which in turns makes us more open to new experiences. It makes us feel more satisfied, which improves our relationships. And gratitude can reduce cortisol (a stress hormone) in our blood, which can ease some physical complaints. The intentional practice of gratitude has been linked a number of positive outcomes[16], all of which lead to a greater feeling of overall wellness.

Peter benefited greatly from a gratitude practice while he was figuring out how to make progress on his screenplay. Before his writing was flowing, he expressed gratitude for the great ideas he was collecting in his brainstorming app. When his words began to flow, he expressed gratitude for every one of them. And when he had his first breakthrough day, he paid attention to the details, and took note of how excited, relieved, and delighted he was to have found his voice again.

Peter used the *Great Work Journal* to support his gratitude practice. Every day, it prompted him to name something for which he was grateful. I encouraged him to dig into the details of what he was grateful for, so that he could activate a specific, emotional memory. Instead of "I'm grateful that I was able to write today," he wrote, "I'm grateful that I wrote 500 words today. It felt like such a relief when I felt myself sink into the zone for the first time in a few weeks. And I loved the dialogue that came pouring out in the second act." These details will allow him to revisit this memory and feel those feelings again, giving him twice the impact from one breakthrough.

At the end of every day, he was prompted to reminisce about his favorite memory from that day. Making the good parts of our life visible through a daily gratitude practice gives us a deep well of memories to visit when we have a hard day and need a reminder of how far we've come. Reflecting on these memories has another benefit, too: You become keenly aware of what you like, what you value, and who you are. This self-expertise will be critical as you work to keep your health and happiness intact while doing your Great Work.

THE TRUTH ABOUT SELF-EXPERTISE: IT'S LIMITLESS

SELF-EXPERTISE IS A BODY OF knowledge that will continue to grow as you pay attention and develop it. If you are experimenting and paying attention, you will discover that you are full of quirky particularities. That's a good thing!

In addition to our Hours of Greatness and our gratitude and wellness preferences, we are particular about when we like to share our work (early and often versus when it's ready), where we like to work (in an organized and optimized office where we have everything we need versus on the move from coffee shop to living room couch to library table), how eating fits into our work schedule (stop working and take a real lunch versus grab food that can be consumed while typing), how we set our boundaries (allowing life and work to intermix, or having hard lines between work hours and non-work hours) and a million other things.

You'll even gain self-expertise about your self-expertise! Gil loves multitasking under some conditions and will begrudgingly single-track under others. Peter checks his email before writing most days, but when the deadline is near, he skips it. I hold rigid boundaries between work and home, except when it comes to things that my kids want to help with. My eleven-year-old daughter, the ever-responsible Abigail, is my fulfillment manager. When I get a new client or a bulk-order for journals through my website, she puts together their package, prints the shipping label, and sends it out. (She charges me one dollar per journal, shark that she is). Because she goes to school during the workday, we do this in the evening when she gets home. Though this violates my usually impenetrable work-life boundary, it's worth it because it allows my daughter to participate in my Great Work, which delights us both.

When it comes to your particularities, don't try to make them make sense to other people. Some people will deeply care about things that other people do not even notice. For example, my husband needs to clean his workspace before he can concentrate, whereas I can work next to a pile of dishes that have accumulated over two days and I won't notice. He can't *not* notice. And we don't have to agree.

And, on behalf of the rest of the world, I must also ask you to stop asking others to make sense to you! I bet if you look at the list of particularities from a few paragraphs above, one of those particularities stuck in your craw. Maybe you had a reaction about something, like:

- "Everyone needs to take a lunch! Not taking a lunch is everything that is wrong with the world," or
- "Science proves[17] that working in an organized space allows our brain to be more efficient," or
- "Better work comes from early collaboration!"

And maybe, just maybe, one of those also gave you some relief: "I'm so glad I'm not alone in my absolute insistence that the office be immaculate before I work."

There *are* things that are likely to work for most people: single-tracking, getting up early, eating lunch. But if you are one of the people for whom these strategies do *not* work, then you've discovered something critically important.

Stop doing those things immediately, and follow that voice of truth instead, no matter what the "experts" say. Because *you* are the real expert on you.

And we're not done with self-expertise yet! The very next chapter opens up a whole new category of self-expertise: how to manage your mind so you can trade defensive failure-- failing by doing nothing-- for productive failure, or failure that comes from doing your Great Work badly (at first!).

CHAPTER SIX

EXCHANGE DEFENSIVE FAILURE FOR PRODUCTIVE FAILURE TO DO GREAT WORK

"You will learn more from a glorious failure than
you ever will from something you never finished."

*Neil Gaiman, best-selling American novelist and
comic book author of richly imaginative and fantastical tales*

WHEN WHAT WE ARE DOING is Great Work, the stakes climb.

Every task is *important.*

Every connection is *significant.*

Every opportunity is *once-in-a-lifetime!*

And failure? Oh, failure is NOT an option!

This can create an incredible amount of pressure and cause us to shut our work down: We might procrastinate when we should be getting started, trip over self-doubt when it's time to persist, and get entrenched in perfectionism when it's time to finish.

These three phenomena (procrastination, self-doubt, and perfectionism) are examples of defensive failure, or the kind of failure that comes from *not doing* what you know you need to do. It is the frustrating experience of not scheduling a mentoring session after someone has kindly offered their time, or getting halfway through a proposal and then putting it down, or refusing to hit publish once the article is written. Defensive failure threatens your progress all the way through your Great Work. My goal in this chapter is to move you out of defensive failure and into *productive* failure.

Productive failure happens when you are *actually doing* your Great Work. Yes, you might be doing it badly at first, but as you ask for help, try new strategies, and learn new skills, you get better over time. Productive failure is not only acceptable and survivable, but is, in fact, *required* for Great Work. Yet there are times when productive failure *feels* like the proof we've been dreading that we don't actually have what it takes. It is the anticipation of this dreaded outcome that sends us back into the throes of defensive failure. And it is this reaction that we are hoping to reverse in this chapter.

DO I HAVE WHAT IT TAKES TO DO MY GREAT WORK?

Diana is a brilliant woman. She's dynamic, creative, funny, curious, and truly dedicated to leaving the world a little better than she found it. She directs the IT team at a boutique financial services company. She was one of the company's founding employees, and she has helped to build it into a regional powerhouse. She's very good at what she does.

Her work in financial services is absolutely part of her Great Work, but lately she's felt like she's run out of things to learn in her role. But, at the same time, she's happy and comfortable and she makes respectable money. She's really not looking for a change. And yet, she is looking for a chance *to grow.*

"I love the work I do, but lately I find myself also wanting to… write." Her voice starts out strong, but ultimately tapers to almost a mumble.

"Write what?" I ask.

"Young adult historical fiction?" It comes out a question.

"Fascinating," I say. "Tell me your idea."

After a few moments of thought, Diana comes alive in front of me. "There's a princess from Romania who was very nearly married off to George the 5th of England, but she refused. Can you imagine turning down the King of England? She went on to be Queen of Romania, but I think the story of how she refused to become the Queen of England would fascinate teenage girls. It was so courageous and so empowering…. The people surrounding her are also very interesting and complex. I think it would be a great novella."

"You should definitely write it! Why wouldn't you?!"

Diana almost freezes, looking at me in her penetrating way for nearly a minute. And then, she physically deflates in front of me. She looks down, covers her eyes with her hand, and massages her forehead.

The collapse is so complete that I ask if she has a migraine. "No, no, nothing like that. I'm just not sure I can write that book. I really want to… I've wanted to for five years. I've read countless books on Marie of Romania, including her autobiography three times. I've watched documentaries... I badly want to write this book. But, Amanda, seriously, I don't think I can."

Diana really has tried. In the five years since she was inspired by Marie of Romania's story, she's done a *lot* of research. She has a file on her computer called "Marie's Refusal—First Draft" which consists of a title page and then pages and pages of notes. She took a weekend workshop, and has since completed not one, but two full outlines.

And yet, in all those many pages, there's not a single line of prose.

Before you become dismissive that she "just didn't want it enough" or "clearly can't prioritize," remember that we are talking about *Diana*. Diana, who manages a large team, is a great mom to two teenaged girls, and is so responsible, she could retire right now. At fifty-two. With no problem.

This woman is a role model. I want to be her when I grow up!

The easy explanation—that Diana must be deficient in some way, or not driven enough, or not organized enough—just doesn't hold up.

There must be more to this story.

There is.

Diana was trapped in a cycle of defensive failure. She was stopped in her tracks, right at the beginning: deeply committed to her project and terrified that she might not have what it takes to do it. At the heart of defensive failure are these competing beliefs:

- We want nothing more than to do our Great Work.
- We never, ever want to find out that we don't have what it takes to fulfill our life's purpose.

It's easy to get fully entrenched in this dilemma, hoping things will resolve on their own. Diana was stuck at the beginning, hoping that she would find evidence that she was already, inexplicably a great writer. Or, alternatively, that she didn't really want to write that novella after all. Either of these would release her from the deeply frustrating experience of defensive failure.

Unfortunately, defensive failure doesn't tend to resolve on its own.

The inconvenient truth is this: The only way to find out that we have what it takes is to get started before we feel ready, stay at it when we want to quit, and finish our projects.

OVERCOMING PROCRASTINATION TO GET STARTED

GETTING STARTED IS OFTEN THE hardest and most drawn-out part of making progress. I know people who have been sitting at the starting line of projects and goals for *decades.* They have book ideas, business ideas, installation art ideas, theories to test, and inventions spinning in their minds. This is their Great Work, yet nothing has happened.

Well, not *nothing.*

They've thought about it. Talked about it. They've even set goals around it.

But then?

Nothing.

Perhaps this nothing is experienced as "goalnesia"—that experience where you set a goal, get excited about it, and then *immediately* forget about it. Maybe you are angling for an exciting promotion that involves managing a brand's social media. "I'm going to post on social media five times this week!" you say, in the hopes of learning digital marketing. And then, you wake up at the end of the week to the fact that you've not even thought about posting, let alone actually posted. This can be a very frustrating experience, because it feels outside of your control, like amnesia.

At other times, you may be acutely aware that you aren't doing your Great Work. Maybe you have a great idea for a children's television show that you just know could be a huge success. What you need to get started is a connection with someone in television who could sanity-check your enthusiasm and help you figure out a couple of next steps.

Hey, great news! Out of nowhere, you learn that someone you knew from graduate school now works in television! You go through the trouble to track down her email address, and then, you actively *do not write* that email every single day for six months.

In both cases—whether you are worrying about it or oblivious to it—you aren't *doing it.* Instead, you're engaged in the defensive failure tactic of procrastination.

Procrastination pops up at the beginning of our Great Work because getting started is the hardest part. Maybe this is because we are at our most vulnerable in our fight to believe in ourselves: All we have is an *idea.* A hope. A wish. A dream, even.

To get started—to do things we haven't done before, that maybe we don't want to do, on behalf of a project that might not work—we must believe more in those ephemeral ideas than we believe the hammering voice in our head telling us that we don't have what it takes.

And we aren't ever going to feel *ready* for that. We will never feel fully certain that the wispy hopes of our Great Work are truer than the loud, self-important voice of our self-doubt. If we wait for that guarantee, requiring certainty of ultimate success before we even start, we will stay stuck. Until we exchange defensive failure for productive failure (or, said another way, until we get into action and stay there despite doing it badly), we will be stuck right here at the starting line... forever.

Our goal, then, is to quiet the panicked voice of self-doubt enough to get started. To do this, we may need to set aside some unhelpful beliefs, or mindset blocks, long enough to get started.

TWO VOICES

Throughout this book, we've talked about the need to listen to the voice of truth in your mind and believe what you hear. And now I'm telling you to believe an "ephemeral idea" over the voice in your head. What gives?

It turns out that we have a couple of voices in our heads, and they are both trying to help us out. One voice speaks in the restraining voice of self-doubt, encouraging sameness, safety, and predictability. This voice is critically important when our physical safety is on the line. The other speaks in the expansive voice of creativity, prompting expression, collaboration, and desire. When we are trying to uncover and pursue our Great Work, we want to privilege that second voice.

At times it can be difficult to tell the difference between the two. To distinguish these two voices, pay attention to how you feel when that voice is speaking.

Do you feel like shrinking into the shadows or hiding away? That is probably the restraining voice of self-doubt encouraging safety over progress.

Do you feel excited and called to adventure? That is probably the expansive voice of creativity calling you to take a risk on Great Work.

WHAT DOES IT TAKE TO SUCCEED? IS IT TALENT OR EFFORT?

WHEN IT COMES TO TRIGGERING defensive failure at the beginning, one of the biggest culprits is the fundamental worry that we *just can't*—not "won't," "will struggle," "don't want to," or "will be humiliated," but that we CAN NOT. Some people can, but, sadly, we are not one of them.

This mindset was first named by Carol Dweck, whose original theory concerned overall beliefs about intelligence[18]. Some people hold the belief that intelligence was given by God or passed down through genetics, and there's nothing more to be done about it. Carol Dweck calls this having a "fixed mindset" which dictates that you don't have what it takes, because what it takes was given at birth. If that's true, it might actually be *impossible* for you to do your Great Work.

Mindsets are collections of beliefs. There is the anchor belief, and then a whole collection of ancillary beliefs that are considered "*also true.*" The anchor belief in Dweck's original theory is about intelligence (intelligence is given at birth), and it comes with these "also true" beliefs:

- Things come easy for smart people. Effort means that you aren't.
- Intellectual risk-taking is dangerous, because other people might see that you aren't smart.
- Asking questions shows others that you aren't smart
- Mistakes provide *proof* that you don't have what it takes.

Of course, you could hold the more positive mindset (what Carol Dweck calls having a "growth mindset")—the belief that intelligence grows through effort over time—and gain the positive impact of that entire collection of beliefs, instead:

- Effort means you've arrived at your evolving edge! This is great news, because this is where growth happens.
- Intellectual risk-taking is how we find the things that will grow us.
- Questions give us shortcuts around common stumbling blocks. Asking questions is a great strategy.
- Mistakes are inevitable, and though they are uncomfortable, they aren't *that big* of a deal.

Though the original theory focused on the concept of intelligence and concerned school children, I have found that the growth mindset / fixed mindset dichotomy is actually highly specialized, particularly in professional adults. One can have a growth mindset about budgeting, for example, and a fixed mindset about communication. We can have a fixed mindset about being organized, athletic, and frugal, while holding a growth mindset about being creative, assertive, and detail-oriented, among hundreds of other traits.

Whether we are worried about intelligence or frugality, when we worry that we don't have abilities that others have, we stack the deck against getting started. These concerns lure us into wasting our time. Instead of doing the work, we procrastinate.

To resolve this mindset block, we need to change the questions we are asking. We need to go from "Can I do this?" to "How can I do this?" We must discover *how* to get on our evolving edge, find the help we need, and put in the time to learn.

I'VE GOT WHAT IT TAKES BECAUSE WHAT IT TAKES IS EFFORT, OVER TIME, WITH HELP

WHEN YOU HOLD A FIXED mindset, you say things like, "I'm just not frugal," or "I'm not an athletic person," or "Some people are detail-oriented, but I'm not. I never have been."

If you have a growth mindset about these things, you say things like "I haven't yet figured out how to be frugal." Or "I haven't found an exercise that I like yet," or "I need to practice being detail-oriented."

Notice that in both cases, the person speaking isn't successful. This is because having a growth mindset isn't about being good at something. There are lots of people with a fixed mindset about how capable they are. "I've always been a words person!" they'll say. Or "Being frugal just runs in my blood."

The growth mindset / fixed mindset question isn't about your success... it's about your beliefs. Is this thing—whether it's intelligence, frugality, athletics, or anything else—something you can develop with effort over time, or do you have to be born with it?

We actually know the answer to that question, because recent advancements in brain science have shown us how our brain works on a fundamental level. In short: Your brain is great at problem-solving; it loves a good puzzle, and will joyfully dig in and figure something out for you. This process is so fundamental that it changes the physical structure of your brain when it happens. New thoughts ignite new neural networks, a phenomenon called "neuroplasticity." Then, your brain is highly motivated to make these new neural networks permanent and efficient, a phenomenon you know as "learning." This is your brain's natural state: learning new things and making them efficient.

The catch is that as much as your brain loves a good puzzle, it *hates inefficiency*... so if *you* don't believe that you can do it (i.e., you hold a fixed mindset), your brain isn't going to play along. It will, instead, disengage. Scientists see this on *f*MRI brain scans as significantly less brain activation for someone with a fixed mindset, and I've seen it again and again as procrastination.

Thus, *you must believe* in your own ability to get your brain on board. And then, you need to expose yourself to challenge, keep at it when it gets hard, and seek help when you get stuck. Trust that your brain can do almost anything—including your Great Work.

So, do you have what it takes to do Great Work? You do, if you are willing to put in effort, over time, and ask for help.

Diana, despite her many degrees and colossal success, suffers from a fixed mindset about writing creatively. When it comes to "intelligence" as a whole and communicating clearly through writing, Diana isn't at all concerned. "I know I'm smart. I can do difficult tasks. And I'm a clear writer when writing to inform, like in reports, or email, or white papers."

And yet she is entirely daunted by writing a one-hundred-page novella. Why? What is Diana struggling to believe about herself?

Diana struggles to hold a growth mindset toward her creativity. She sees a stark difference between the kind of clear, concise writing she does at work and the creative process of fiction writing that involves creating a whole world from scratch, just from her imagination. And yet, creativity, like intelligence and frugality, is something that grows through effort over time with help. The struggle to express yourself creatively triggers neuroplasticity, which triggers learning, which triggers greater creativity. When you run into a problem you can't figure out, you ask for help, which triggers neuroplasticity, which triggers learning, which triggers greater creativity. Over time, with effort and help, you *develop* your creativity, and your intelligence.

Knowing this can calm our self-doubt long enough to allow us to get into the flow of our Great Work. This helps us to get out of defensive failure and into the more satisfying (though still frustrating) experience of productive failure.

The full resolution of the fixed mindset / growth mindset block, regardless of what you are struggling with, comes from *experiencing* progress. You won't fully believe you can save money until you've changed your habits and begun to build some savings. Diana won't believe she can write creatively until she's sat down and hashed out a first draft. It's the process of failing and improving, of stumbling and getting back up, that allows us to experience the remarkable progress that comes from effort, over time, with help.

The first step, then, is to set aside your worry long enough to set a weekly task and a daily to-do, and then do them. Make them small, so small, in fact, that you can't feasibly argue that failure would be that bad. Diana, for example, could set a timer for fifteen minutes and write one scene she doesn't intend to use. Doing something this small would give her a new experience, which would begin to rewrite the story she's telling herself about fiction writing.

You may worry that such small tasks will never accumulate into the accomplishment you are seeking. But never fear! Over time, your tasks and to-dos will get larger and more significant. Your skills will improve and your Great Work will accumulate.

I'LL NEVER BE ALBERT EINSTEIN

HERE'S A CONVERSATION I HAVE had with many clients, students, and people who hear me speak on these ideas. Let's name my conversational partner: Ruthie.

> **Ruthie:** "Amanda, aren't people different? Some people are more athletic, or more frugal, or more creative, or better at math."
> **Me:** "Yes."
> **Ruthie:** "So, how can you say that anyone could be Einstein, or Kobe Bryant, or one of those hyper-frugal people who forage for all their food?"

Me: "That's not what I said. You don't need to be Kobe Bryant to get in shape. You don't need to be Einstein to do math, and you don't need to forage all your food to be frugal. And you're right, you probably won't ever be Einstein. And that has almost no impact on your ability to do everything ordinary people do every day. If ordinary people are doing it, you can, too. With effort, over time, and with help."

Diana didn't need to be the very best young adult historical fiction writer of all time. What she wanted was to spend time with some characters, empower some girls, and share a cool story.

Normal people do that all the time!

So could Diana, which is what I told her.

We discussed neuroplasticity, looked at brain scans, and figured out that the *only reason* she wasn't yet rocking her creativity was because she wasn't yet willing to get started and fail on the road of "good enough."

That's when she got choked up. Because it turns out that in addition to holding a fixed mindset about creativity, Diana does NOT want to be the kind who gets involved in failures for the sake of art.

I AM THE KIND OF PERSON WHO DOES THIS... BECAUSE I CHOOSE TO BE THAT KIND OF PERSON

DIANA HAD A DIFFICULT CHILDHOOD. Both of her parents have substance-abuse issues, and there was never any money. Home life ricocheted between all-consuming chaos and almost total neglect. After her parents divorced, her mother, a writer and sometimes painter, remained absent for weeks at a time. Then, abruptly, a crisis in her mother's life would consume every waking moment of everyone's life. Life at home was volatile and unpredictable—two things that school, for Diana, was not.

"School was my safe haven, my ego boost, my chance to shine. Learning wasn't hard for me. I could do well just by showing up. With a little hard work and some basic follow-up, I was a great student. Top tier: valedictorian, lots of scholarships and opportunities... all of it.

"Being a high achiever got me some appreciation and attention that simply wasn't available at home. I took every opportunity to be praised ... I was the president of the art club and captain of the debate team. I turned in school projects that went way above and beyond. In sixth grade, I wrote a three-page paper on Van Gogh that talked about his early life and hypothesized that a childhood illness was responsible for his lifelong struggle with mental illness.

"This was what I turned in when I was asked to complete a worksheet with questions like, 'What is one interesting thing about Van Gogh's life?'

"I realize now that this, like so many other over-the-top efforts, was just so someone, somewhere, would see me and tell me I was good enough. Unlike my mother, I was responsible, reliable, and hardworking. That piece of my identity was my life-raft out of chaos, and I was desperate for someone to validate it."

Diana has done a lot of work to overcome the damage she sustained in her childhood. She's been in therapy for years. She's had healing conversations with her parents, and she's faced her own trauma head on, and she is, as mentioned previously, a total rock star.

And yet, the legacy of this commitment to proving that she is responsible and hardworking above all else lives on in her identity. And it was this piece of her identity that was causing her to struggle to write her novella.

IDENTITY SHAPES BEHAVIOR

IDENTITY IS A POWERFUL CONCEPT. The foundation of our identity is created in childhood and reflects, largely, the way our parents and caregivers saw us. "Mom says I'm creative. I agree." Or "Dad says I'm a great writer, so OK, I buy it." I think of this primary identity as fifty percent a result of who we semi-objectively are (personality traits, tendencies, preferences) and fifty percent the luck of the draw, based on how well our parents and other caregivers were able to see us and support us.

We carry that primary identity into adolescence, where the job becomes what psychologist Erik Erikson[19] calls "identity fracturing." This is a normal part of adolescence, where we reject pieces of our identity and take on pieces of new identities. Through this painful and tumultuous process, a coherent identity emerges. This is who we know ourselves to be as adults.

Our identity then operates as a filter for the world; when something matches our identity, it's easy enough to do. When something is in tension with our identity, it can feel almost impossible. This is called "an identity-based mindset block." Our job, in this case, is to make some room in our identity for what we want to do.

"I'm just not a creative, arty, free-spirited person," Diana said.

What is it about being creative that conflicts with Diana's identity? It's probably not the bare-bones notion of doing creative work. She wrote a voluntary three-page paper on Van Gogh, for Pete's sake. She wants to be a writer. She has annual memberships to three art museums. Clearly, she's not against art. So, what's the problem?

Remember how I said that mindsets are *collections* of beliefs? Though the mindset is anchored into a core belief (i.e., "I'm not a creative person"), it's linked to a lot of other beliefs that feel related to Diana. Her own description of "free-spirited, arty people" hints at the beliefs she has bundled with creativity. When probed, Diana says, "I don't know... I feel like creative people are often kind of flighty... they sleep late... they don't make any money... and they aren't particularly responsible." It's these *related beliefs* that were bothering Diana. This is possibly because they reminded her of her mother, who was a creative and free-spirited person who also struggled to be responsible and take care of her family. Who wants to be creative if you have to be broke and irresponsible? Not Diana, that's who.

If she becomes flighty, irresponsible, and stops making money, she reasons, her husband will feel betrayed. Her friends will feel like they don't know her anymore. And, because her

family of origin was harsh and unforgiving, transgressions like these feel extremely dangerous. The unstated concern of most identity-based mindset blocks is: *If I'm not who my family, friends, and colleagues think I should be, my whole life could fall apart.*

Identity-based mindset blocks are most powerful when they are unexamined. When Diana sits down to write the novella, her brain will cycle between two unexamined and competing commitments[20]:

- On the one hand: "I want to write this novella."
- On the other: "Writing this novella puts me at risk of being irresponsible, flighty, and broke."

These two competing commitments will battle it out, behind the scenes, until she's too conflicted to do anything at all. As we discussed, competing commitments need to be resolved to break the cycle of defensive failure and get you into action.

To resolve a competing commitment, we must ask the unasked questions. For Diana, they sounded like these: "Do you think you can write your novella while still being you? Might it be an asset when writing historical fiction to be organized, good at research, and an early riser? And are you planning to quit your job next week and only write this novella?"

The answers shone a clear light on the unexamined beliefs that were blocking her progress. This eased a great amount of tension in Diana, making it possible for her to start her novella for the first time.

Just to be clear: Diana wasn't *ready*. She wasn't sure that she would succeed. But she was sure enough, and ready enough, to try. And that's as ready she needed to be.

Resolving competing commitments allows us to begin to re-write our stories, but it's staying in action that allows us to move beyond the mindset block for good.

Diana already had her vision (to be a writer of YA historical fiction) and her accessible aspiration (to write the novella), so she set a ninety-day goal (write three chapters, one per month).

She worked through her nerves through weekly tasks (such as, "Write a first draft of the first chapter,") and daily to-dos (such as "Finalize the Chapter 1 outline.").

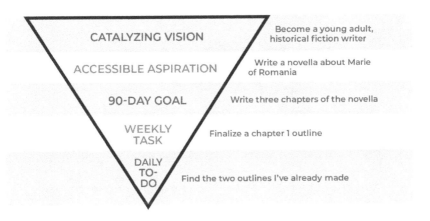

As she made progress by being her usual responsible self, joined communities of writers and enjoyed their company, and met other people in the publishing world who appreciated her just as she was, Diana's mindset block resolved itself. It turns out that if you are yourself, doing the thing you want to do, you realize that you *can be yourself and do what you want to do!*

Taking weekly and daily action in the real world, unlike all the affirmations and mindset mantras in the world, allows us to move past the assumptions that are holding us back. For Diana, she learned that those "related" character traits don't have to be part of creativity. This allowed her to relax into the belief that she was a creative person.

Of course, she didn't get it all right! Her first draft of her first chapter was 10,000 words (that's really long!) and she self-reports that her dialogue was "stilted and way too obvious." But she was on her way: She traded defensive failure for productive failure, and she got some traction. And it felt amazing.

IDENTITY VERSUS GROWTH

These two mindset blocks (growth and identity) can sometimes sound like the same thing. This is because we often use the same words to describe each. For example:

"I'm just not a math person" can be shorthand for both a negative identity *and a* fixed mindset. The difference is that a fixed mindset is undergirded by the belief that "Some people are math people, but I'm not. Since I don't have what it takes, I should never have tried." The solution here is to understand that math (or whatever you are holding a fixed mindset about) is not about talent or genetics. It's about effort over time with help.

Compare this to "I'm just not a math person" in the identity sense. It's undergirded by beliefs like "Math people are boring, linear, humorless, and probably actually robots." This one is about the mismatch between what you believe about yourself and the people who carry this identity. The solution is to allow yourself to be seen in a new way, and to drop the connected character traits that are the real problem. We can be good at math without being a humorless robot.

PERSISTENCE: STAYING WITH OUR GREAT WORK WHEN IT GETS HARD

ONCE YOU'VE TRULY GOTTEN STARTED on your Great Work, you have accomplished something remarkable. To begin a vulnerable project that matters to you is an exercise in willpower and courage, and you are truly to be admired! You can never finish an important project if you don't start it.

Now, it's time to learn how to stick with your Great Work when it becomes difficult. And it will get difficult!

- Maybe you are studying for a licensing test and have failed twice already. Should you read the writing on the wall and give up?
- Perhaps you've submitted your work to be featured in magazines ten to fifteen times. Every time, you get the same form letter back thanking you for your interest in their work, but due the large volume of submissions… blah, blah, blah. Should you move on with your life?
- Maybe you've applied for literally dozens of jobs in the field you want to work in and gotten exactly zero calls for an interview. When do you let it go?

There are two answers to all of these questions. First, if the thing you are doing *isn't* critical to your Great Work or your status as a functioning adult, I would refer you to Chapter 3 and suggest that you let it go.

On the other hand, if this thing you are doing matters to you and is critical to your Great Work, then the only option is to persist.

Listen, when the work you are doing is hard, vulnerable, or public, there will come a moment when it's clear that *the only rational thing to do* is quit. You are going to want to walk away.

And other people are going to agree with you! They'll suggest that you do something safer, closer to home, less difficult, and more predictable. They'll point out that odds are stacked against you and argue that the sane thing to do is to give it up. And you will agree with them as they agree with you.

I like to think of this critical juncture as when Defensive Failure tries to lure me back under its spell, with a creepy ghost-like voice. "Come back to procrastination, Amanda! There's a great new series on Netflix, Amanda! You could be perfectly happy without Great Work, Amanda!"

When this happens (which it does, all the time), I force myself to persist.

Persistence, according to the dictionary on my computer, is "obstinate continuance in a course of action despite difficulty or opposition." I love that they use the word "obstinate," because it denotes such a strength of conviction. "Everyone (including myself!) told me to quit, but still, I persist!"

That's the way real persistence feels—against all odds and driven solely by the courage of your commitment. When I look at the difference between the people who are doing their Great Work and enjoying its rewards and those who just sit around wishing they could do it, I notice exactly one difference: The people doing it are *doing it.* Even when it's hard. Even when they are embarrassed, disappointed, and afraid. Through insurmountable, impossible, and inevitable odds. When it seems very unlikely that they will ever get it right.

The key to Great Work is to keep going. When you run into a roadblock, which you absolutely will, it's time to tune into your obstinance and persist.

PERSISTENCE DOES NOT MEAN "BANGING YOUR HEAD AGAINST THE WALL"

Now that we've agreed that you are going to persist, I want to bring some common sense into the conversation. There is a difference between persisting at your Great Work and persisting *in a strategy* that simply doesn't work for you.

It's inevitable that some of your efforts will be really different from what you imagined. When we are dreaming of our Great Work from the safe confines of procrastination, we think that everything is going to be lovely, interesting, and satisfying. But over here in "persistence-land," parts of it are hard, boring, and unsettling, instead.

Everyone doing Great Work has started down a road that ends up being a bad fit:

- You are trying to pass your licensing exam and have been working with a video course and workbook, because your partner says that preparation courses with an instructor are a "colossal waste of money." But you can't concentrate on any more videos!
- You've been trying to submit your work to magazines, and you aren't getting any traction. The worst part is that you aren't getting any feedback, either! You've toyed with the idea of putting your articles on a blog and sharing

with your social networks, but your MFA advisor always said that blogs aren't real publishing.

- You want to change fields and get a new job. You've applied to SO. MANY. JOBS, but you aren't getting any bites. You've considered trying to get a job in your current field doing work that is more transferrable, but you worry that you would be settling.

In each of those examples, there is the larger goal to which we are committed: passing an exam, getting our writing out in the world, and moving our career forward. But the strategy we are using to get that goal *isn't working*. Even though other people have made it work, it simply isn't working for us.

Usually, when you are trying to force yourself to do something that is a bad fit, it means you're trying to persist through largely extrinsic motivation. You are trying to do it the "right way," which others would agree with, instead of the way that works for you. And that's not going to be enough to keep you going when things get hard.

- If the strategy we are using isn't critical to our Great Work or is one of many paths to the same place, it is probably time to move on.
- Find the funds and hire a tutor, or find someone who is just getting started as a tutor in this space and trade time. Maybe you are just someone who needs to have a living, breathing human to ask questions.
- Go ahead and blog, blog, blog! As your ideas get out into the world, you will quickly learn what interests your reader and what doesn't jive. Plus, maybe your blog will

catch the attention of an editor. That's how I ended up with my first published article, as a matter of fact.

- Follow your instincts, and look for a job that requires you to stretch on skill set, but not on field. Set goals, tasks, and to-dos to get as much out of your new role in your old field as possible. Then, you can look for another job with your new skills in a year. You don't have to be in a hurry.

It's important to realize that changing our strategy doesn't mean that we are giving up on our Great Work. Instead, we're just acknowledging that persistence requires self-expertise, too! The sooner you let go of a strategy that doesn't work for you, the better. If you don't, you might confuse your strategy with your Great Work, and end up quitting for good.

REASSURANCE FOR PERSISTENCE

There will be times when you will feel disappointed, disheartened, exhausted, and maybe even miserable. You might question your sanity, because who in their right mind would put themselves through this?

During these times, it's easy to forget how much you've done, how far you've come, and how hard you've worked. Instead, you feel as though you have accomplished *nothing* and gotten *nowhere,* and the only rational thing to do is to *quit.*

When this happens, I would like to refer you back into the pages of your *Great Work Journal*. Right there, day after day, you will see the progress you have made:

- Daily to-dos, done!
- Weekly tasks with progress made!
- Favorite memories to make you smile.

Your work in the *Great Work Journal* provides you with a living record of your successes. At times like these, you need that. And once you've reassured yourself that you are not the raging failure you worried you might be, please take a break.

Taking a break is not giving up.

It's not procrastination, and it's not defensive failure.

It's taking a moment to recharge your smile and renew your commitment. It will make all the difference in the world when you return to your Great Work.

I WANT TO DO THIS ON MY OWN TERMS

As DIANA BEGAN TO MAKE progress on her novella, she noticed a troubling pattern: "I enjoy the ins and outs of writing... but when I come to an impasse and need to dig through a hard part, I seem to stall out instead. When this happens, weeks can go by without much progress... it's very frustrating."

"What's happening when you find yourself stalling out?" I asked.

"It's usually when I get to a sticky part of the story that I just can't figure out, or a difficult edit that I'm not sure what to do with. Really, any time when I need to slow down and just dig through it and figure it out."

"What kinds of thoughts are you having when you stall out? What are you complaining to yourself about?"

"I don't know... mostly *I don't have time for this, I have so much work to do, I can't afford to be consumed by this, why am I spending all my free time on this...* mostly thoughts about time."

Diana wants to engage in her Great Work. But she's struggling with how to do so in a manner that doesn't violate her other commitments, in this case her commitment to her career and her downtime. The worry is that she'll spend so much time writing that she may miss something at work or overwork and become tired. And this slows her down and causes her to stall out.

These kinds of worries can make our Great Work feel a little dangerous:

- I want to be a professional speaker, but only if I can do it in a way that doesn't take me away from my family.
- I want to train for a marathon, but only if it doesn't damage my body.
- Or the premise of this book: I want to do Great Work, but only if I don't have to sacrifice everything else.

If you look at each of the examples above, you might recognize two competing commitments situated right in the center:

- I value professional speaking, and I value my family.

- I value long-distance running, and I value the long-term health of my body.
- I value great work, and I value balance, relationships, and happiness.

The solution here is to resolve the competing commitment by rejecting the assumed conflict between your commitments and setting some terms.

I want to do this, *and* it must not violate these boundaries.

For Diana, her competing commitment was that she wanted to write the novella (desperately), but she's also very dedicated to her career and her downtime. She worried that she would get caught up in the novella and fall behind or get frazzled. She felt this pressure most when she needed to spend extra time with her novella to figure something out.

She worried that if she went all-in, as we do sometimes need to temporarily do to get past a stumbling block, she would be swept away, taking all her free time and career security with her. That was unacceptable, so she disengaged instead.

It was frustrating to her that she couldn't just push through and keep her pace. She began to worry that she didn't have the long-term persistence to stay with it, a re-emergence of her fixed mindset. But of course, that's simply not true. Instead, she just needed to set some terms to allow herself to invest time in her project without worrying that she was opening herself to something reckless.

I asked her: "What commitments and reminders do you need to keep on hand so you can feel safe enough to dig in and stay with it?"

She came up with: "I'm going to re-commit to some boundaries. I will write for one or two hours a day before work, as I have been. No more than that on a workday. Then, and only if I really need to, I'll add one three- or four-hour block on weekends. I think that will give me the extra time I sometimes need, without the risk of losing all my family time to it. And I can always remind myself that real progress comes from consistency and not brute force."

This same process of making commitments to ensure that we are doing things on our own terms can help with any of the examples above:

- "I will pursue professional speaking up to six gigs a year. Then, I'll take a break and re-assess with my partner."
- I will begin training for a marathon but will meet every other week with a physical therapist to ensure that my body is handling the strain.
- I will use the guardrails from the *Great Work Journal* to make progress while still actively prioritizing my health, happiness, and family.

Making these kinds of explicit commitments allowed Diana to feel more in control of where she was headed—a helpful feeling when persisting in the face of setbacks.

ASK FOR HELP, DANG IT!

When we run into a roadblock, it's often the case that a switch in strategy, or a new mindset is needed.

These can be difficult to see on your own!

A coach can point out where you could be misinterpreting what's happening.

Maybe you are stuck between two choices. A coach can help you uncover a third option that you are ignoring.

Perhaps you are deeply entrenched in a strategy that isn't working. A coach with experience can help you craft a better strategy.

Often, a coach is most helpful when you feel like quitting because a coach will always believe in you, even when you lose your own confidence.

I have a tiny little enclave of six accidental entrepreneurs (like coaches, experts, and creatives) that I help to do their Great Work. If you would like to consider working with me, I'd love to hear from you[21].

If I'm full, or can't help you, I will send you a list of high-quality coaches and therapists who are familiar with the Great Work Method.

TIME TO WRAP IT UP: PERFECTIONISM'S PLAYGROUND

WHEN YOU RESOLVE COMPETING COMMITMENTS and begin to work from helpful instead of restraining beliefs about your Great Work, you open the door to progress. Suddenly, it's much less difficult to get around to filling out your *Great Work Journal*, to writing that truly terrible first draft, to asking for help when you need it, and to prioritizing what works for you.

Plus, there's much less procrastination, shame, fear, hurry, hustle, worry, and guilt. They ease, because you're clearer in your own mind.

And then you start to fly.

You are making progress like a boss, handling setbacks like a pro.

In fact, you're almost done!

Now, you just need to send the book to the editor, hit "publish" on your video, send the resume, make the phone call, or share your ideas at the meeting.

But there's one thing you forgot to do. One part that could be improved. One more run-through would calm your nerves. One more read-through, just one more.

We have arrived at defensive failure's last stand.

You've overcome procrastination and gotten started.

You've gotten flexible with your strategies and overcome the desire to quit.

Now, you just want everything to be *perfect*. Is that so much to ask?

Actually, it is, because perfection is an impossibility.

Perfectionism is continuing to hammer away at your project long after you are seeing meaningful improvement. It usually involves things like wordsmithing perfectly good text, and obsessing between two very similar options instead of just picking one. It's not long before you trade "better" for "different," and it's official: You're stalling.

It's time.

Right now.

Let. It. Go.

Diana was blown away by how much progress she made. In fact, she finished that novella. And then finished it again. And finally finished it one last time.

"I had done so much research, and it was important to me to do a thorough job. I just kept adding more context and developing the characters more. Then I edited, and edited, and edited. Finally, I hired a book coach who guided me through the mechanics. It was the editor that finally convinced me that it was done. I'd probably still be editing if it weren't for her!"

As the editor worked to convince Diana that her novella was complete, Diana struggled to believe her. Something so monumental that she had struggled with for so long—how could it be *done*?

Recently, Diana sent me an email. It read: "My editor convinced me to send it off to a literary magazine. 'Just to get some feedback,' she said. And then, Amanda, you won't believe it! I found out today they are going to publish it as a serial! I am *so* excited!"

The novella was ready. And with help, so was Diana.

TRUST YOURSELF AND YOUR ABILITY TO DO GREAT WORK

IT'S REMARKABLE HOW TANGLED WE get in our minds. Mindset blocks, unexamined, competing beliefs, and identities we don't even know we have, all compete to take us off track. It's hard to do Great Work with defensive failure around every corner!

And defensive failure is even more prevalent than it seems because we are always starting, persisting, and finishing, across all the dimensions of our lives, and within each dimension across several projects. In addition to her writing, Diana had projects at work and at home that were starting, persisting, and finishing.

The process of Great Work is not linear. It's multi-faceted, with different parts of the work starting, persisting, and finishing all at the same time. If her writing was going swimmingly, she might be trying to launch a new initiative at work. If she was coasting at work, she might be struggling to support her daughter through a tough time at school. And, of course, there are times when the writing was stuck, she had a new project at work, and trouble was brewing at home. Because life is complex and multifaceted, so is Great Work.

In fact, let's name it for what it is: Great Work is *messy*. The irony of it all is that this mess is part of what makes it so satisfying! If it were easy, it wouldn't be invigorating. If it wasn't complex, it wouldn't captivate us. And if it didn't matter (and, as such, couldn't make us feel vulnerable and afraid), we wouldn't care.

The message for Diana—and for all of us—is this: You *can* do this. When you desire something, when you really yearn for it, it's because you are meant to live it. To learn from it. And to develop into *more of yourself* because of it.

As you choose helpful beliefs over restrictive ones, let go of false identity associations, discover your path to persistence, and find the courage to put your work out there in the world when you are *almost* (but not entirely) ready, you will do Great Work.

CHAPTER SEVEN

YOUR GREAT WORK IS CALLING YOU

I, LIKE MOST HELPER TYPES, had some serious scarcity issues when I first started my business. I was socialized (as a woman, as an academic, and as an employee of non-profits) to think that if I loved something, I should be happy to do it for free. This was causing my business to fail, and I needed to fix it. So, off I went to a two-day workshop about money mindsets.

Toward the end of the workshop, the facilitator asked us: "What's your craziest dream?"

People came up with all kinds of "crazy dreams," like:

- Make five million dollars in my business.
- Be on TV as a guest expert.
- Write a best-selling book.
- Sell my company to Google.
- Share my message with a million people (that was mine).

And then the facilitator asked the follow-up question: "Has anyone else ever done this?"

In every case, of course, the answer was "*Yes.*" Many, many people make millions of dollars in their businesses. There are about 500 books on the *New York Times* Bestseller list every year[22]. And Google's holding company has acquired more than 200 companies, according to Wikipedia[23].

So, "yes," we reported dutifully. People *are* doing these things.

"Well then, why not you?" she asked. "If someone is going to make five million dollars, why not you? If someone else can sell their company, or be on TV, why not you?" Then she looked right at me (I remember it like it was yesterday), "If some other schmuck who isn't a psychologist, without an infectious silly streak, who doesn't get fired up like you do, can get his message out *to a million people*... why, Amanda, not you?"

It hit me like a thunderbolt. *Why not me?*

I realized that by letting this idea be my "craziest" idea, I was making it feel impossible. I was putting it on a pedestal and keeping it at bay. I needed to change my ways, or I was never going to get what I wanted.

First, I acknowledged that getting my message out to a million people was a vision: a "someday, somehow" kind of idea—exciting, but not really actionable.

So, I worked that vision down through the levels.

Accessible Aspiration

If my vision was to gain access to a large audience, then what was my accessible aspiration? What could I do in the next year or so to get me closer to that vision? Since I already enjoyed speaking, I decided I would work for the next year to get booked regularly for free speaking engagements. At least once a month sounded doable.

90-Day Goal

Given that my accessible aspiration was to speak regularly, what stretch goal could I set for the next ninety days to get started? I already knew some people who ran networking groups and thought that I might be able to get a few of them to book me. I decided to aim for three or four bookings in the next ninety days.

Weekly Task

Now that my goal was to get three or four bookings in ninety days, I needed to do something this week to move me closer to it. I decided to write a couple of emails to the people I knew who ran networking events.

Daily To-Do

To send these emails, I was going to need email addresses. One of the people I knew from way back in 2002 when I was doing professional development workshops in Massachusetts just after college. We were Facebook friends, but I hadn't spoken to her directly in more than ten years. So, I set time aside to look at her Facebook page and catch up before searching for an email address.

CATALYZING VISION — Get my message out to ONE MILLION people!

ACCESSIBLE ASPIRATION — Speak regularly on psychology and work, at least once a month.

90-DAY GOAL — Get booked to speak for free 3 or 4 times.

WEEKLY TASK — Write two emails to people I know who run networking groups.

DAILY TO-DO — Find that email address from 2002.

I made many consecutive 90-day goals, spanning a year or more and comprised of countless weekly tasks and daily to-dos. I booked myself to speak in front of groups of ten, fifteen, or forty people. "Speaking to a few people this week is better than speaking to no one," I reasoned.

When I had spoken to twenty groups, I set the goal of getting accepted to a TEDx stage. I applied to a lot of TEDx stages, and mostly heard nothing. I just kept applying, though, certain that something would eventually come through.

After I had spoken to about thirty groups, I set the goal of completing Heroic Public Speaking's Grad School[24], a powerful training program for aspiring professional speakers. Their tagline is, "Change the World One Speech at a Time." Obviously, this was a great fit for me, but it was a huge expense at the time. I hemmed and hawed and wrung my hands about it for a full six months. I remember the sweaty palms and racing heart when I gave them the credit card for my deposit.

It was *terrifying*, but I'm really, really glad I did it, because just after enrolling, I learned that I was accepted to speak on the TEDx Harrisburg stage in just a few short months.

A coach at Heroic Public Speaking, Mike Ganino[25], worked with me one-on-one to prepare. He helped me make it funnier, cleaner, more compelling, and easier to understand. I revised and then rehearsed it in front of anyone who would sit still long enough to listen. Abi, my daughter, listened to it as a bedtime story on more than one occasion.

Before I knew it, it was time.

I traveled from my home outside of New York City to Harrisburg on Sunday, October 14th, 2018, and I gave it everything I had.

I enjoyed every one of the sixteen minutes I spent on that TEDx stage. My husband and a good friend came to watch, along with about 150 other people in the audience. The crowd laughed at my jokes (despite how it sounds on the recording!) and nodded along to my stories. When I got off the stage, people came up to me and told me that my message had inspired them.

It was a *great day.*

And that was enough.

The crazy thing about TEDx is that you go there, do your talk, and then hear *nothing.* For months. I knew it would eventually drop to YouTube, but I'd heard estimates from other TEDx speakers that it can take between four and nine months to see it uploaded to the TEDx YouTube channel.

About four months later, in February of 2019, my phone started buzzing with text messages.

"I saw your TED Talk. It's amazing!"

"How are you getting so many views?"

"Hey, I love your talk! Why didn't you tell me it was coming out today?"

That is how I found out that my TEDx talk had dropped to YouTube[26]. By the time I saw the video, it had 3,000 views. I was *blown away.* The views climbed quickly, reaching 10,000 people by the end of the first week.

By June of 2019, it had 500,000 views, and in August of 2021, it hit one million views.

Along the way, the video has received hundreds of comments and maintains a 98 percent thumbs-up ratio. Most people who comment are grateful for my message of hope.

So, to recap: *I shared my message with one million people.*

My "craziest" dream came true.

Why not me, indeed.

My real point, here, though is *why not you?*

There is nothing special about the people doing their Great Work out in the world. They are just people *who are doing* their Great Work!

They are doing exactly what we've covered in this book:

- Getting clear on their vision and then making those Great ideas actionable by setting goals.
- Doing less to make space for Greatness.
- Taking action every week and every day while developing self-expertise.
- Handling the inevitable mindset blocks, defensive failure, and competing commitments along the way.

You can do these things, too.

GREATNESS IS NOT GUARANTEED, BUT IT IS MORE LIKELY

THE STORY OF MY SUCCESS with my TEDx talk is to help you understand that greatness is possible, even for us mere mortals. But I don't want you to think that it was all sunshine and rainbows!

I got rejected from *at least* six other TEDx talks.

I did a live rehearsal in front of a networking group the week before my TEDx talk and went entirely blank. I couldn't remember a single word! I was so. very. embarrassed… and terrified. What if this happened on the day of my TEDx talk? Cue *all the drama.*

While I was on stage at TEDx, my bra strap slipped down my arm *twice.* I pushed it up, and then it fell again. So, I pushed it up a second time.

This means that ONE MILLION PEOPLE have seen my bra strap. And trust me, the people of YouTube want me to know. Most of the comments that aren't about how much they like the talk are discussing the bra strap.

And let's be real! My TEDx talk is moderately popular, but I'm in *no way* famous. Brené Brown's TEDx talk has fifty-five million views. I'm a small fish.

Here's my point: Nothing is ever perfect. And fortunately, nothing *has to be perfect* to be really, really great.

Doing your Great Work does not guarantee greatness. It doesn't guarantee fame, wealth, notoriety, or a full book of business.

What it does guarantee (and I think this is better), is that you will feel *alive.* You'll be on your evolving edge, learning things that matter to you, connecting with cool people doing awesome things in the world, and being a role model for the people looking at you with admiring eyes. Honestly, the feeling of doing Great Work is its own reward.

That said, you are much more likely to achieve greatness if you are doing your Great Work!

GO FORTH AND DO YOUR GREAT WORK

YOU NOW KNOW EXACTLY HOW to do your Great Work.

You know the power of doing less.

You know how to make your great ideas actionable, and you won't be surprised when you fail along the way.

You know how to develop self-expertise and manage defensive failure.

There's nothing left to do but start. Persist. And finish.

I have no doubt that taking these exact steps will allow you to do great things in the world, and I hope you'll share your excitement with me. I'm just an email away.

Oh, and one final word of encouragement:

You've got what it takes.

And it's time.

APPENDIX

GOALCABULARY

B- Work: This involves completing tasks when they are "good enough" *and no better*. B- work relies on a practice of relentless imperfection, and can save you scores of time on tasks that no one cared about in the first place.

I've decided to do B- work by keeping my receipts in a folder on my phone instead of in a complex receipt management system. If I get audited, I've got what I need.

Defensive Failure: The failure that comes from *not doing* what you know you need to do. This failure is defensive in that it is deployed to prevent productive failure.

Procrastination, perfectionism, and distraction can all be signs of defensive failure.

Goalcabulary: A list of unusual or unfamiliar terms related to Great Work and goal setting.

I learned a lot of new goalcabulary from the excellent book "Great Work."

Goalnesia: The phenomenon where you set a goal and immediately forget all about it.

I intended to go to the gym twice this week, but because of goalnesia, it didn't cross my mind again for three weeks.

Gratitude: A three-part process that reinforces the good things in life, which can make you happier and healthier.

> **Anticipation:** Gratitude for things that you hope and expect to happen. Creating positive feelings in advance allows you to get the full benefit of the anticipation.
>
> *I imagined the look on my soon-to-be husband's face as I walked down the aisle. It filled my chest with anticipation, almost causing me to cry.*
>
> **Savoring:** Gratitude for something that is happening right now. Paying close attention to details provides a strong memory trace upon which to build further reminiscence.
>
> *As my daughter walks across the stage to graduate, I savor her confident stride and head held high. I watched her face break out in a smile as she held her diploma, and as her face turned to search the crowd for me.*
>
> **Reminiscing:** Gratitude for what has already happened.
>
> *I like to reminisce about the day I finally got to swim with dolphins. The sun was so warm, but the water was so cold! I didn't think I would feel nervous but I did. Then once I was in the water with the trainer, I just relaxed and loved every minute.*

Great Work Thread: A way to name the commonality that brings together your most moving experiences, natural interests, and the things that spark your curiosity. It can include any or all of the following: issues that matter to you, fields or sectors that fascinate you, particular tasks that you enjoy doing, and your unique way of being in the world.

My Great Work Thread runs through creative expression, educating curious learners, and making things fun. I know that to be happy I need to have an outlet for all three.

Levels of Goal Setting: A hierarchy that helps us to know how best to move our ideas forward, and helps us ascertain whether an idea is something we should act on now or put in the parking lot for later. Each level has both a recommended timeline and a next step.

> **Vision:** A mental image of what you hope your future will be like "someday," created through brainstorming and listening to your hopes, dreams, and desires. Vision acts as a magnet, drawing you toward opportunities and projects that get you closer to your desires, and helping you to say "no" to opportunities and projects that don't. To move a vision forward, activate it.
>
> *Anna's vision for her life involves being an influencer in the national conversation about therapy, veterans, and the role art can play in healing the traumas of war.*
>
> **Accessible Aspiration:** Projects that you hope to bring to fruition over the next one to two years. Accessible

Aspirations need to feel both exciting and doable. To move an Accessible Aspiration forward, keep it in your mind while setting your 90-day goals.

Anna's Accessible Aspiration is to start a non-profit. She knows it will take multiple 90-day goals and a lot of figuring out to get there, but she's certain that with effort and persistence, she can do it.

90-Day Goals: Intentions for the next ninety days, which will guide how we set our weekly tasks and act as guardrails to ensure we stay focused on our intentions. To move a goal forward, set weekly tasks.

Anna's goal was to re-activate and build her social network in the veteran's service industry. Specifically, she wants to have at least twelve conversations with people in this space.

Weekly Tasks: Intentions for the coming week. These usually take effort over a few days, but can be accomplished in a week. To move a weekly task forward, set daily to-dos.

Anna's weekly task was to reach out to her connection at the Wounded Warrior Project.

To-Dos: The things you intend to do today. The to-dos should advance your weekly task, which advances your 90-day goal. Once you've done your daily tasks, you can rest easy, knowing that you are taking your dreams seriously. To move a to-do forward, do it.

Anna's to-do was to find the email address for her connection at Wounded Warrior.

Mental Contrasting: A powerful goal-setting theory developed by Gabriele Oettingen which prompts us to ask, "What could go wrong?" and then plan our way around that roadblock, every time we set a weekly task or a daily to-do. This theory is built into every level of the Great Work Journals.

Mental contrasting helps me to be less frustrated because I'm never expecting things to go as planned. It has made me more patient in general and I've made much more progress.

Motivation theory: A theory that hypothesizes that our interest and motivation can influence us in two distinct ways.

>**Intrinsic motivation**: Interest that is born inside of you. It's grounded in interest, driven by curiosity, and connected to your hopes, dreams, and aspirations.
>
>*Intrinsic motivation is the kind of motivation we typically feel about our Great Work.*

>**Extrinsic motivation:** Interest that comes from outside of you. It's grounded in expectations, tied to approval and regulation, and sometimes driven by worries, fears, and scarcity.
>
>*The work we do while motivated in largely extrinsic ways is at best "fine" and at worst shallow and poorly executed.*

Parking Lots: Holding zones for projects, goals, tasks, and to-dos that have value and merit, but aren't priority right now.

Long-Term Parking: A holding zone for projects that you are excited about and want to get to someday, but you don't have a realistic timeline for the project now. Projects can remain in long-term parking for years.

I know that I'd like to play the piano, but I'm too busy to take lessons or learn about it now. I've put "learn piano" in the long-term parking lot.

Medium-Term Parking: A holding zone for projects that are coming soon but can't be advanced for the next couple of months at least. Projects in medium term parking tend to be either taken up as goals, or moved to long-term parking within a year.

Updating my online course is a great idea, but I can't get to it during this 90-day cycle. I'll put it in medium term parking and consider it for the next ninety days.

Short-Term Parking: A way to remove something from your active involvement by putting it out of your mind for a few hours, a weekend, a week, or a month. Projects in short-term parking are often actively underway, but a short hiatus creates space for other important projects or priorities.

I am putting my entire career in short-term parking for the next two days while I enjoy my family trip to Vermont to go leaf peeping.

Productive Failure: Action-driven, insight-filled productive failure comes from doing something badly at first.

Unlike defensive failure, productive failure is a necessary step on the road to mastery.

The Productivity Roller Coaster of Doom: A cycle of destruction wherein a person engages in extreme overworking until he or she experiences a period of total exhaustion and burnout, which leads them to rest until they recover slightly. At this time, the person returns to a state of overworking.

I spent three years on the Productivity Roller Coaster of Doom, endlessly cycling between overworking and exhaustion.

Rash-hole: Someone who allows their own preferences and inclinations to dominate collaborative work. Though it's important to develop and express our self-expertise, it's critical that we also take the timelines, preferences, and needs of others into account, too.

The quintessential rash-hole is the person who cancels the meeting at the last second because the agenda "doesn't feel in integrity" with their vision, despite that ten other people have already arrived and the catering is on the way.

Self-Care Tactics: Two categories of things that help us to feel resilient, happy, healthy, and joyful.

> **Fortifiers:** Involve ensuring our baseline health and resilience. This usually involves moving and resting our bodies, eating good food, getting enough rest and downtime, and spending at least some time in the company of other

people we enjoy. Out of this category of self-care comes mental, emotional, and cognitive health.

When I am rested, fed, and feel connected to my family and friends, I know that I'm fortified enough to do Great Work.

Invigorators: When we experience at least a baseline threshold of fortified health and wellness, we begin to yearn for things that excite us. This can involve adventures to new places, opportunities to eat new food and try new activities, or projects that challenge us to dig deeper and contribute more.

I find Great Work to be one of the greatest invigorators of them all!

Self-Expertise: Expertise about how you, specifically, make change. Self-expertise helps you to optimize your work flow, timing, collaboration practices (and much more!) to your specific tendencies and preferences. This allows your Great Work to flow with more ease and paves the way for rapid progress.

Everyone says that you should "eat the frog" and do your hardest work first. My self-expertise tells me that I make the most progress when I do my most fun, deepest, creative work first. I'm following my self-expertise, even though it contradicts traditional wisdom.

Vision Activation: The process of "amping up" your vision with details and specifics that make you feel excited, hopeful, and invigorated. Doing this makes your vision more compelling and more magnetic, helping you to do be more courageous in your pursuit of it.

I activated my vision by imaging myself standing on the stage at Lincoln Center, receiving my lifetime achievement. As I imagined the look on my children's faces as they clapped for their mother, it made me want it so badly that I was ready to do whatever it takes.

ACKNOWLEDGMENTS

NOTHING IN MY LIFE HAPPENS without the enduring support of my favorite people: the Crowells. David's protective "Mommy's upstairs writing, leave her alone!" made space in our pandemic life for creation. Abigail's hug deliveries (delivered against the orders of her dad) kept me connected, even when I was deep in the words. Alexander's dramatic readings of chapters allowed me to hear what I could no longer see. We made this book together, as we do all things.

The team that has supported this book has been nothing short of awe-inspiring. Michelle Pariza-Wacek and Megan Yakovich who dug me out of my entrenchment and got me writing again. AJ Harper, editor extraordinaire, who adopted me into her Top Three Book family and treated me as one her own. Sincere thanks to Anna Paradox, who took my "final" draft and fixed it (she's going to ask me to delete those quotes!). Total gratitude to CB Messer, who made a book that looks exactly how I wanted it to. The best part of this book has been getting to know all of you, and appreciating your expertise.

Thank you to my advanced readers, Nora McCormick and Linda Charnes. Your feedback made everything better.

A special long-time-coming thank you to those who believed in my ideas before I did: Alisa Libby, PJ Podesta, Sarah Todd, Jenni Avins, Teri Thompson, Deanna Kuhn, and Chris Schunn.

With gratitude to the teams of educators who exposed me to many of the key ideas in this book: Michael Rothman, Alicia Wolcott, Aaron Boyle, Jessica Furer, Tony Bryk, Paul LeMahieu, Anna Kawar, and Alicia Grunow.

With deep appreciation for my support network: Alyssa Adams, Meghan Bathgate, Sara Beall, Val Bullerman, Caitlin Faas, and Monica Moore.

With love to the people who made me: Grandma, Grandpa, Dad, Mom, and Ryan.

ENDNOTES

[1] You can find all three Great Work Journals on Amazon. If you would like to make a bulk order to use with your own clients, give to your team, or send as gifts, please reach out to me directly.

[2] The World Health Organization upgraded the definition of burnout in the new version of its handbook of diseases, the International Classification of Diseases—ICD-11—which went into effect in January 2022. You can find the updated definition here: https://icd.who.int/browse11/l-m/en#/http://id.who.int/icd/entity/129180281

[3] David Allen's book *Getting Things Done* (2001) (GTD) is an outright phenomenon in time management and productivity circles. There are apps, blogs, notebooks, and communities build around GTD and its component parts, such as inbox zero.

[4] To learn about how growing the world's largest pumpkin can be a part of Great Work, check out Mike Michalowicz's book, *The Pumpkin Plan*.

[5] To learn more about the Four Forces Framework and download a copy of Trish Blain's book, *The Four Forces of Everything*, visit nonordinary.com

[6] For more on how visual activities can release us from the super logical, hyper-verbalized part of our brain where self-doubt reigns king, check out the first part of *Drawing on the Right Side of the Brain* by Betty Edwards.

[7] Senge's book, *The Fifth Discipline,* is a great exploration of how shared vision can drive an organization's growth and success. I find that his arguments for organizations are very useful when thinking about an individual's vision as well.

[8] For more information, consider Todd Herman's concept, The 90 Day Year.

[9] Researchers call this ego depletion. The classic study was done in 1998 by Baumeister, Bratslavsky, Muracen, and Tice (in the Journal of Personality and Social Psychology, 74, p. 1252-1265) and many other studies have confirmed and expanded these findings. For a review of the research, consider Inzlicht and Schmeichel's 2012 review paper in Perspectives on Psychological Science, 7(5), p. 450-463.

[10] For a great exploration of process goals and habit formation, read James Clear's book, *Atomic Habits.*

[11] Gabriele Oettingen's theory is a direct response to "positive thinking," which she suggests can sabotage progress by setting unrealistic expectations. You can read more about this in her book, *Rethinking Positive Thinking.*

[12] To learn more, read Rubinstein, Myers, and Evans's article in the Journal of Experimental Psychology, (27(4), p. 763-797), Executive Control of Cognitive Processes in Task Switching.

[13] Gil is referring to a concept advanced by Cal Newport in his book *Deep Work,* which argues that our best work is done in a state of distraction-free focus. This state, when extended, can result in work beyond our typical cognitive capabilities.

[14] *Savoring: A New Model of Positive Experience* is a great, if dense and technical, book about the positive psychology that can enhance a gratitude practice.

[15] For a deep dive on negativity bias, consider Rozin and Royzman's 2001 review article, "Negativity Bias, Negativity Dominance, and

Contagion," in the journal, *Personality and Social Psychology Review*, 5(4) p. 296-320.

[16] To learn more about the research and applications of gratitude you can read any one of Robert Emmons' books. If you are new to reading psychological research, I recommend starting with his popular press book, *Thanks! How the New Science of Gratitude Can Make You Happier.*

[17] Science never "proves" anything. We know that, right? Science supports, refutes, and adds nuance... but no scientist would ever say that something is "proven." Gravity is not proven. Molecular structure is not proven. So, I can assure you, absolutely nothing in the realm of productivity is "proven!" If you hear experts say that "science proves I'm right," they don't understand science, and you should be deeply suspicious of them. If some regular person says that science proves something, be nice. How are others supposed to know any different, when experts and journalists go around saying it all the time?

Most of all, don't question your emerging self-expertise because "science" has "proven" you wrong. All these experts are really saying is that lots of people, lots of the time can benefit from this strategy. And if you don't, you don't. Listen to yourself and believe what you hear.

[18] You can read much more about Carol Dweck's work in her book *Mindset: The New Psychology of Success,* or you can watch one of her many Ted Talks.

[19] Erik Erikson is a theorist you'll see in any child development or personality development textbook. His original book, *Childhood and Society,* is an interesting starting point, and there are many more modern extensions of his theory, including James Marcia's identity development theory and specific theories focused on the role that race, gender, and sexual orientation play in identity development.

[20] Competing commitments are a concept introduced and explored in Lahey and Kagan's book, *Immunity to Change.*

[21] Check out my coaching page at amandacrowell.com/coach-me/

[22] Yucesoy, B., Wang, X., Huang, J. *et al.* "Success in books: a big data approach to bestsellers." *EPJ Data Sci.* 7, 7 (2018). https://rdcu.be/cEsMR

[23] Alphabet Inc's (Google's holding company) Wikipedia page: https://en.wikipedia.org/wiki/Alphabet_Inc.

[24] Learn more about Heroic Public Speaking on their website, heroicpublicspeaking.com

[25] Learn more about Mike's coaching on storytelling and speaking at mikeganino.com

[26] Watch my TedXHarrisburg talk here: https://www.ted.com/talks/amanda_crowell_3_reasons_you_aren_t_doing_what_you_say_you_will_do?language=en

ABOUT THE AUTHOR

DR. AMANDA CROWELL IS A cognitive psychologist, speaker, author, and the creator of the Great Work Journals. Amanda's TEDx talk: *Three Reasons You Aren't Doing What You Say You Will Do* has received more than a million views and has been featured on TED's Ideas blog and TED Shorts. Her ideas have also been featured on NPR, Al Jazeera, The Wall Street Journal, Quartz, and Thrive Global. Amanda lives in New Jersey with her husband, two adorable kids, and a remarkable newfiepoo named Ruthie. She spends her days educating future teachers, coaching accidental entrepreneurs, and speaking about how to make progress on Great Work to colleges and corporate teams. To book Dr. Crowell to speak or inquire about coaching, check out amandacrowell.com or email amanda@amandacrowell.com.

Printed in the USA
CPSIA information can be obtained
at www.ICGtesting.com
LVHW020050291023
762411LV00010B/29

9 781737 374190